it's
about
time

find 5 extra hours each week

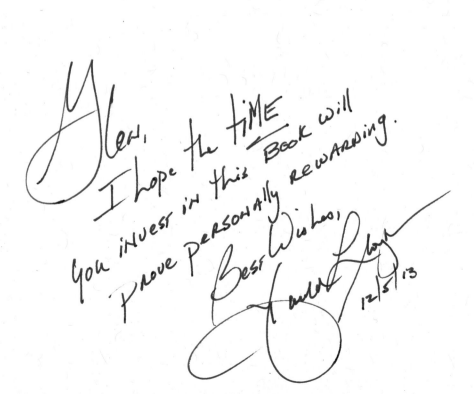

Glen,
I hope the TIME
you invest in this Book will
prove personally rewarding.
Best Wishes,
[signature]
12/5/13

it's
about
time

by harold c. lloyd

find **5** extra hours each week

BRIGANTINE MEDIA

It's About Time

Published by: Brigantine Media
211 North Avenue, Saint Johnsbury, Vermont 05819

Jacket and Book Design by: Jacob L. Grant

Printed in Canada

ISBN 978-0-9711542-9-2

Other Brigantine Media books include:
Am I the Leader I Need To Be? by Harold C. Lloyd
The Big Picture: Essential Business Lessons from the Movies
by Kevin Coupe and Michael Sansolo
Business Success in Tough Times by Neil Raphel, Janis Raye, and Adrienne Raphel
Win the Customer, NOT the Argument by Don Gallegos
Selling Rules! by Murray Raphel
Crowning the Customer by Feargal Quinn

For more information on these books, please contact:
Brigantine Media
211 North Avenue, Saint Johnsbury, Vermont 05819
Phone: 802-751-8802
Email: neil@brigantinemedia.com
Website: www.brigantinemedia.com

Dedication

To all of you who have said on multiple occasions,
"I wish this day had 25 hours."

Acknowledgements

This book started as a seminar designed to help the hundreds of people who had told me over the years that they wished they could find the time to implement some of the good ideas they may have heard during one of my business seminars.

Fortunately for me, the folks at Cornell University enjoyed the seminar enough to invite me to make it into a book for their famous Distance Education Program.

I was truly honored and began to write. Sixteen months later, the first edition of this book was born. Marcia Mogelonsky and Janelle Tauer were the forces behind the creation of that early edition.

Fourteen years later, I realized my book on Time Management made no reference to email, PDAs or Microsoft Outlook, and was in serious need of an update and overhaul.

Good fortune came my way again in the form of Brigantine Media. Janis Raye and Neil Raphel saw my work as an oldie but goodie and pledged to help me make it new again and well worth the time to read it.

My college-aged daughters, Deanna and Randee, donated part of their vacation time to offer their generational viewpoints to help bring this book further into the 21st century. I was proud of their active interest in this project. It was valuable to have their counsel and to incorporate their "20-something" perspectives.

I sincerely hope you benefit from the countless hours of work it took to complete this new edition, the primary objective of which is to help you reclaim five unproductive hours each week, enabling you to redeploy them in a more effective manner to better enhance your life.

Contents

CHAPTER 1

Finding Five More Hours

*"Don't put off for tomorrow
what you can do today,
because if you enjoy it today,
you can do it again tomorrow."*
– James A. Michener, American author

HOW DO YOU VISUALIZE time? Most of us tend to think of time as circular, as in a clock's face, the hands going around and around. But that's not really an accurate depiction. Time is actually linear, like an arrow. Once it passes you by, it doesn't come back.

How about saving time? That's another misconception. Time can't be saved like pennies in a piggy bank. You can't store up the minutes to use later. So let's not talk about saving time. No matter what we do, time gets spent, not saved. We'll show you ways to manage time better, to get more out of every minute and not waste time on meaningless activities.

Where Are Your Five Hours?

I'm convinced that there are at least five unproductive hours each week out there, just waiting to be reclaimed. If you're like most people, you waste at least five hours every week because of poor time management. This book will help you find where you are mismanaging your time and what you can do to take back those five hours.

Think what you could do with five more hours every week. That's one hour of working out Monday through Friday. That's five dinners with the family. That's a long afternoon at the baseball park. That's dinner and a movie with your spouse. That's enough time to paint the shed. That's time for antique-hunting. Or golf ball-hunting. Or job-hunting.

You get the idea. Your goal, and the purpose of this book, is to find those five hours and make them yours. The way to do this is to consider how you're spending each workday and identify what you could change. This book will give you the tools you need to improve your time management skills.

Alex and Logan

Throughout the book, we have illustrated each chapter's concepts with an example drawn from two aspiring businesspeople: Alex and Logan.

Alex is the manager of a large family-style restaurant. He has worked his way up to management after learning the restaurant business from both the kitchen and the front of the house. He's waited tables and been a short-order cook. Alex is full of enthusiasm and experience, but he has plenty of issues when it comes to managing his time effectively.

Logan works for a large insurance company. She's in her first management position and wants to succeed in her new role as supervisor of the department. But her business training in college didn't include anything about managing time.

Alex and Logan need to find those extra five hours, too. Their problems at work may sound familiar. But they're learning, and so will you!

> " Time is what we want most, but what we use worst."
>
> – William Penn, early American colonist

How Organized Is Your Business Life?

Answer yes or no to each question.

1. Do you read mail the first thing in the morning?

2. Do you believe in a total open-door policy – anyone, any time?

3. Are you frustrated that your to-do list never gets completed?

4. Would you rather do it yourself to make sure that it gets done right the first time?

5. Do you immediately say yes to most requests made of you at work, especially those made by a supervisor?

6. Do you hold meetings that don't include an agenda?

7. Do you recruit new employees only when there is an opening?

8. Is disciplining or terminating an employee a task you try to avoid at all costs?

9. Do you regularly fantasize about how nice a nap would feel?

10. Have you found your working hours increasing over time?

Score 0 for every yes answer, and 10 points for every no. And here's a chance to earn some bonus points:

I do in fact:

- Wear a watch   (+ 3 points)
- That works   (+2)
- And is set ahead 5 minutes   (+5)
- Carry a pad and pen   (+3)
- And use them   (+2)

Add it all up. If you scored less than 60, you undoubtedly need some time management help and this book.

Wake Up and Smell the Coffee

As each day passes, your lifeline gets shorter. I don't want to scare you, but it's true. Time is a scarce resource. And continuously depleting.

Try this exercise. It woke me up to the urgency of personal time management:

Write down what you consider to be a really big number. (Ninety percent of people asked to do this write "one million." Most of the rest write "one billion." Financial types write "one trillion." Computer people write "one googol" – that's 10 with 100 zeroes behind it, to the rest of us number-challenged folks.)

Next, write down your age. Subtract your age from 78, the average life expectancy in the U. S. (Source: Centers for Disease Control and Prevention, May 2009). Multiply the result by 365. This number approximates the number of days you have left to live. For example, if you are age 40, subtract that from 78 to get 38. Multiply that by 365 to get 13,870. Statistically, you have about 13,870 days left, my friend.

Compare the number of days left in your statistical life with the big number you wrote down earlier. It's a pretty small number compared to one million or one trillion or more, isn't it? Most people are shocked to find that they have more dollars in their savings account than they have days left in their living account.

Sorry to be so dramatic. But knowing the number of days you have left to live is probably the best motivator you have to get started learning to manage your time better.

IT'S TRUE !

Tom Schmutz, President, Retail Operations and COO at Norrenberns Foods, talks about how he envisions his internal "life clock":

"In the first half of our lives, many of us live with very little concern for our time. We think we will live forever and never grow old. At some point, which is different for everyone, the 'life clock' reaches its halfway point and starts to measure how much time we have left to live, counting backwards. Really good time managers figure this out very early and live their lives accordingly."

It's About Time...

...we learn to take better control of our time. Let's begin the search for those five underutilized hours and figure out a way to redeploy them more constructively.

CHAPTER 2

Slicing Your Pie of Life

"I am miserly with my time in some areas so that I can be profligate with my time in other areas."

– Stanley Marcus, former President, CEO, and Chairman,
Neiman Marcus department stores

Before you can start to find your extra five hours each week, it helps to have a clear picture of how your time is currently allocated. The week has 168 hours and everyone divides that time according to his or her needs and interests. Picture the week as a your favorite flavor of pie. The pie gets sliced into parts to represent the amount of time you spend each week on work, family, and you. Optimally, the pie is sliced into three equal parts: your work time, your family time, and your sleep time. A fourth, smaller sliver is left over for personal development.

Here's how I divide my pie of life:

◆ **Work (55 hours):** All activities directed by the paycheck-providing organization. Five ten-hour days,

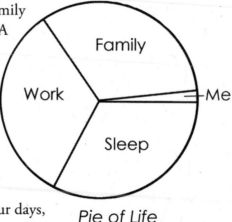

Pie of Life

either at home or at the workplace, plus five hours for commuting or for a sixth day of work.

◆ **Family (55 hours)**: Family meals, household chores, recreation, and spiritual activities. Calculated as almost eight hours per day, seven days a week.

◆ **Sleep (55 hours)**: All forms of rest, including power naps or powering-up breaks. Slightly less than eight hours a night works for me.

◆ **"Me" time (three hours)**: Time spent on educational, spiritual, and physical development, or even goof-off time. This can include college classes one night a week, tennis lessons, meditation—whatever recharges your batteries and keeps you energized. You can use these hours any way you want—that's the point.

Total: 168 hours.

There are 168 hours in everyone's weekly pie of life. How does your pie get divided?

Naturally, everyone's needs are different. Maybe you sleep more or less than I do. You may work out for 90 minutes every day instead of my 30-minute daily run. If you are younger or older than I am, your family time needs may be different from mine, too. But the important idea is that everyone needs balance in life. You can slice the pie anyway that works for you, but YOU should make the choice of how big or how small each slice needs to be.

Imagine a checking account in your name with 168 hours deposited in

> People who cannot find time for recreation are obliged sooner or later to find time for illness."
>
> *– John Wanamaker, American retailer*

it. Keep in mind your three major responsibilities: Work, Family, and Me (including sleep). If you overspend hours in one category, you place at risk the viability of the other two. But if you spend your hours judiciously and keep things in balance, all three entities have a fair chance to thrive. Your division of your pie may change when work demands are especially heavy. That's okay. Just keep in mind the need for balance among the three major areas and you'll quickly get your slices more equal again.

"Pushing the envelope" or "living on the edge" are accepted and even revered phrases we use to describe our exciting lives. But when you're on the edge all the time, it's easy to fall off. We see it every day with people who push themselves too hard and ultimately can't handle the stress. Maybe you've seen this in yourself. It's time to take control of your time, recognize that everyone's pie of life only has 168 hours each week, and take charge of dividing those hours in a more balanced way.

> " Your time is limited, so don't waste it living someone else's life."
>
> – *Steve Jobs, founder, Apple Computer*

Questions to Ask...Yourself

My motto for working has always been, "Love what you're doing at least 70 percent of the time you're doing it, or make a career change." It just doesn't make sense to spend so much time on a job you don't enjoy and so little time each week with your family, friends, or a hobby that you love.

Nothing is sadder than people who, at the twilight of their lives, feel regret for the road not taken. What prevented them from doing what they wanted to do?

There are two possible answers. First, these people probably had no personal plan for their lives that allowed for the accomplishment of a dream or desire. Second, their time management skills were never developed enough to help them find the time to do what they wanted.

You need to be sure you're on the right track. Ask yourself two questions: "Am I satisfied with my life so far?" and "Am I having fun yet?"

If you answered yes to these questions, keep doing what you're doing. But if you answered no to either one, ask yourself one more question: "Have I outlined three goals I'd like to accomplish in the next three to five years?"

Make sure these aren't just professional goals, but ones for your personal life, too. Many people set goals for their careers, but allow their personal lives to drift without direction or focus.

Goal-setting alone is not enough. Your goals must be viable. Can you really achieve your goals? To test the viability of your personal goals, you must be able to answer yes to three more questions:

◆ Do I really, *really* want to achieve the goal?

◆ Will people important to me be involved in the achievement of this goal?

◆ Am I physically, mentally, and financially capable of achieving this goal?

A positive response to these questions will yield almost certain goal achievement. You must have the desire (question 1). You need support to carry you through, especially during any low points (question 2), and you must be practical when selecting your goals (question 3).

> ❝ Every six months, I review where I spend my time. Is it on things that are still important?"
>
> – Art Jones, former President & CEO, Associated Grocers

Take Time Away from Work

At Bobrick Washroom Equipment of North Hollywood, California, a 500-employee manufacturer, employees are expected to leave work in time for dinner. After 5:30 p.m., hardly anyone is still at the office—intentionally. Mark Louchheim, president of Bobrick, says that employees who stay late often reveal poor work habits. "We worry about whether they can delegate properly and prioritize their work," he says.

A study published in the October 2009 *Harvard Business Review* confirms the value of taking time away from the job. Hard-driving management consultants were asked to stop working at 6:00 p.m., and do no work for the rest of the evening. The study found that requiring people to take time off work helped them plan ahead, streamline their workloads, and focus better while on the job. According to the authors of the study, Leslie A. Perlow and Jessica L. Porter, the consultants found it hard at first, but the rewards on the job were worth the initial effort to change their habits. After five months of "predictable time off," surveys showed that the consultants involved were more satisfied with their jobs and their work-home life balance, and clients reported that the work level had improved.

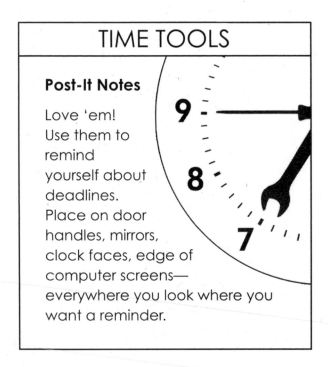

TIME TOOLS

Post-It Notes

Love 'em! Use them to remind yourself about deadlines. Place on door handles, mirrors, clock faces, edge of computer screens—everywhere you look where you want a reminder.

Sue Shellenbarger, a reporter for the _Wall Street Journal_ who wrote about the Harvard study, implemented the practice in her own work schedule. She forced herself to have at least one work-free day every weekend. This was a new idea for Shellenbarger, but one that worked well for her. She reported that she used proven time-management principles to keep her work-load in check and on track.

You can do the same for yourself. Set a schedule that forces you to declare part of your weekends or evenings work-free. Stick to your schedule of predictable time off, and soon you'll find that you are more productive while you are at work. You still need to get the same amount of work done, so you'll force yourself to use your time at work more efficiently. In the process, you're likely to improve your over-all work performance as well.

> " The most important gift is time."
>
> – _Tracey Smith, creator of International Downshifting Week_

Downshifting

The search for balance in life is known as downshifting. It's a trend to-ward a simple, less money-driven life. A Gallup poll showed that twelve percent of people who were stressed at work would prefer to work fewer hours for less pay. Half that number of non-stressed people would pre-fer to do the same.

Meaningful work and a balanced life are deep-rooted human needs. They can be ignored for some period of time, even years, but eventu-ally, they will beg for your attention.

I am not advocating devoting less time to your job than is needed, tak-ing a cut in pay, or minimizing your commitment to your responsibil-ities. Rather, look for ways to make yourself happier and enrich your life on and off the job. Sit down in a comfortable chair and read Elaine St. James's *Simplify Your Life: 100 Ways to Slow Down and Enjoy the Things That Really Matter*. Brush up on your guitar picking. Take a course on a topic that has always sparked your interest.

If you can't downshift, daydream. To you and to many people today who are hooked on their PDAs, this may seem like an absurd, unproductive waste of time. But researchers are finding that the opposite is true. As you think about what's next, your daydreams may hold the answers. Daydreaming can help you tap into your childhood reflections of your original vision of yourself that may have gotten lost in the shuffle of your life. When you daydream, you scan current situations and develop creative solutions to those problems. Ultimately, daydreaming can help you become the person you want to be. Daydreaming is like visualization for athletes. Seeing something in your mind helps you reach your goal.

Daydreaming can be a way to relieve stress and regain balance and perspective. You just might find it redirects your focus, leading you in whole new directions toward opportunities you never thought existed.

Live Your Priorities

Don't wait until the twilight of your life to realize that you have ignored the important things. If you have difficulty saying no to people who try to rob you of your time, remember that the time they take from you is gone forever. You must assert self-discipline to protect your priorities and maintain your balance. Try this exercise. Make a list of your life's

> " The tragedy in life doesn't lie in not reaching your goal. The tragedy lies in having no goal to reach."
>
> – Benjamin Mays, American educator and scholar

priorities, in order of importance. Here's my list:

1. Loving and guiding my three children
2. Achieving physical fitness
3. Furthering my education
4. Helping retail organizations maximize their potential
5. Traveling the world with my lovely lady
6. Writing a third book
7. Taking great care of my home
8. Performing more community service

Make your own list and then make three laminated copies. Put one list on the wall in your workstation, office, or work area. Stick another up by your bathroom mirror, and put the third by the home phone that you use most often. The office list is to remind you of your life priorities when work demands become overwhelming. The bathroom list is to make sure you think about these priorities every day. Maybe you'll daydream over them while you're brushing your teeth or taking a shower. And the list by your home phone will really help you when you get those calls that put you on the spot. When someone phones to ask you to volunteer, supervise, or partic- ipate in anything, glance at your list of priorities and de- cide which item on that list would be served by getting in-

> " A vacation is what you take when you can no longer take what you've been taking."
>
> – Earl Wilson, athlete

volved with the new task. If it doesn't fit into one of your priorities, dis- cipline yourself to decline the request, politely but firmly. In effect, the request would be robbing you of the time you would want to spend elsewhere. And it's probably time you can ill afford to lose.

Give Each Day an Identity

Give every day of your life a unique identity. For example: "This is the day I am going to start my new book," or "Today is the day I'm giving Jennifer her performance review," or "Today's the day I'm going to draft an outline of my year-end report." When each day has a special identity you treat each day more meaningfully and with more respect. It's likely that all your day's activities will take on more significance because they must be conducted within the framework of making sure the unique event is completed successfully.

"Just another day" is an expression of the bored, the boring, or the unproductive. How can one get excited for an event held during "just another day?" By assigning a unique identity to each day, that day acquires a special flavor—not just plain vanilla.

Summary of Chapter Two:

Before you start to learn how to manage your time at work better, step back and evaluate how you use your time today. What are your general life priorities and how does your work fit with those? Are you truly happy at work and in your life? If you're not satisfied with the picture you see, it's time for a change.

Make sure you are slicing your pie of life into pieces that give you balance. Too much of anything is usually not a good thing, whether it's too much work, sleep, or personal time. "Moderation in all things" is a valuable maxim that can help guide your time management.

How to Evaluate Your Life's Time Management:

1. Consider how much time you devote to the major portions of your life: work, family, and yourself. Are they in balance?

2. Determine major life goals as well as professional goals. Make sure they are achievable for you.

3. Try imposing a schedule of taking time away from work. This may help you be more productive during your working hours.

4. Slowing down or daydreaming are worthwhile pursuits for people who spend most of their time at work. Pulling away from the rat race can refresh and recharge your engine, and can help you visualize how to meet your life goals.

5. Prioritize your list of objectives, and use those priorities to guide how you use your time. Don't take on tasks that don't fit with your priorities in life.

6. In your mind, give each day a unique identity that sets it apart from any other day and makes it more meaningful.

TIMELESS ADVICE

Grab hold of the 24 hours you're given each day.
Allocate them like you would any other
precious, limited resource.

CHAPTER **3**

The 20-Minute Disappearing Act

*"You must master your time
rather than becoming a slave to the constant
flow of events and demands on your time."*
– Brian Tracy, author and speaker

*M*onday morning, 8:00 a.m. Alex, the manager of Marie's Restaurant, pulls into the parking lot to begin his shift. He worries about being "piranha-ed" again this morning by his staff. "Every day," he thinks, "there are at least two servers, one prep person, and one cook lying in wait for me when I come in the front door." Alex wants a little quiet time before his day at work begins, but the piranhas never give him the chance.

As he enters the restaurant, the feeding frenzy begins. First, the head chef. "One of the refrigerators is acting up again," he says. "We had to move everything into the other box, but when the delivery comes in today, there won't be enough room." Alex remembers that he had meant to call the refrigerator company to have a service person come in and have a look before the warranty expired. He'd written himself a note to that effect, but somehow it had disappeared on his paper-strewn desk.

Next up, the supervisor of the wait staff grabs him and sinks in her fangs. "Two of my servers have called in sick today and I don't have any back up to replace them," she complains. Alex thinks, "We were supposed to have *a meeting to work out an action plan to organize the servers' schedules—what happened to that?" He makes a few quick phone calls to get replacements, and makes a mental note to hold that meeting with her ASAP.*

After getting the server problem solved for now, Alex moves on to the next item in the restaurant that needs his immediate attention. "No quiet time again today," Alex thinks. "I wonder what it would be like to start out with a few minutes of planning for the day before my bones are picked clean by the piranhas?"

Are You Being "Piranha-ed"?

The first hours of any businessperson's day can be extremely hectic. Everyone has questions, needs, problems that must be solved right away. Where is that report that was due yesterday? Have the early morning deliveries been recorded and sorted? What happened in the Kansas City office overnight?

No matter what type of business you are in, what hits most businesspeople when they walk through the door are issues that must be handled immediately. Nothing gets the adrenaline flowing like seven crises fully under way as you walk through the door to start the day.

Let's be honest—many managers enjoy the excitement or the ego charge associated with demands requiring their immediate attention, especially those inevitable emergencies at the beginning of the day. Everyone wants to feel needed, and a group of people vying for your time is a sure way to establish your importance. But for the managers who know how to manage time—both their own and that of their employees—there is no reason to accept that the piranhas must attack every day.

Start your journey toward better time management by making time for yourself. You can't take charge of anything that goes on at the workplace until you take control over your own schedule. What could be more debilitating to a productive day than to begin it by running around in dizzying circles?

The 20-Minute Disappearing Act

The first strategy of time management: disappear for the first 20 minutes of your day at work. Whether you start your day at 7:00 a.m., noon, or midnight, reserve the first 20 minutes for yourself, with no one else able to interrupt. This will give you a good chance to get organized for the day. It will enable

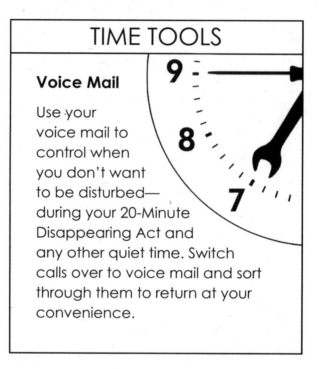

TIME TOOLS

Voice Mail

Use your voice mail to control when you don't want to be disturbed— during your 20-Minute Disappearing Act and any other quiet time. Switch calls over to voice mail and sort through them to return at your convenience.

you to provide direction for the people who depend on you for leadership. As one businessperson described it, "I block out a time early in my day to have a meeting with myself." It doesn't mean that the usual daily calamities associated with business will cease, especially those that seem to lie in wait for a manager about to start the day. It just means you won't participate in those feeding frenzies until you're ready to handle them.

In the first 20 minutes of the day, you set your pace for the whole day. During those few minutes, the productivity level for you and your staff is determined. So how can you to protect this very precious period of time? The best thing you can do is to disappear for 20 minutes.

What do you do in those first 20 minutes? One manager we know uses the first 20 minutes of his day to straighten out his desk and prioritize the jobs he wants to accomplish. Another manager spends her 20 minutes enjoying the silence of her office and mentally anticipating the day ahead. The key to a successful 20-Minute Disappearing Act is to use the time to get your thoughts in order, decide what your priorities are, review important appointments, and figure out what you want to accomplish throughout the day. These first 20 minutes, if used correctly, will be the most important minutes of your day.

Abracadabra!

Disappearing acts are hard enough for magicians to learn. How does a businessperson master the trick?

Here's the secret: go to the place where you have the greatest control over distractions, and make sure the place is logistically convenient for you. Your office may be the place for your 20-Minute Disappearing Act *if* you can be assured that no one will be able to disturb you there. A booth at the restaurant across the street or the coffee shop around the corner might be your best spot to disappear. You may find, as many managers do, that the ideal place for your 20-Minute Disappearing Act is the front seat of your car as you drive to work—as long as you turn the radio and the phone off! The point of this exercise is to think and to organize your day without distractions. A great song might get you bopping along, but not necessarily in the direction of your job. Save music for the drive home to put you in the right mood for your reunion with your dog, guinea pig, guppies, or your family.

> " For every minute spent in organizing, an hour is earned."
>
> – Benjamin Franklin, American founding father

You must make every effort to treasure and protect your first 20 minutes. If you schedule your 20-Minute Disappearing Act before the official start of your workday, you'll have a much better chance of using the time for the intended purpose—to plan and organize for the day ahead. There are plenty of ways to "disappear" at the start of your day, and when you've found the one that works for you, stick with it.

Planning Your Day

The 20-Minute Disappearing Act gives you the time to create your schedule for the day. You may want to use a paper planner, your PDA, or a free online calendar like Google Calendar or iCal. First, take a look at what's on your calendar for today, and note the fixed commitments you already have—a meeting with your boss, a training session for new employees, your son's dentist appointment—and begin by writing these into your schedule. Now, review the medium and long-term goals that you are working toward (i.e. improving customer relations, making your meetings more impactful, or leaving your office at 5:00 p.m. on the dot.) Doing this will help you decide which tasks are most important and which interruptions that will inevitably occur deserve your attention.

Pull out today's to-do list. Figure out which tasks you can throw out or delegate to someone else, which tasks you must do yourself, which tasks you must accomplish today and which tasks can wait until another day.

> " I learned that we can do anything, but we can't do everything, at least not at the same time. So think of your priorities not in terms of what activities you do, but when you do them. Timing is everything."
>
> – Dan Millman, author, speaker, and former world trampoline champion

Now fill in most (not all, because a certain level of interruption is un-avoidable) of the space left in your workday with the tasks you plan to accomplish today. Give the more important tasks precedence to be sure you don't overlook them.

Complete a Small Task

During your 20-Minute Disappearing Act, find a way to accomplish a small but meaningful task. Starting your day with a sense of accomplishment sets you on a positive track for the rest of the day. SOAR during your 20-Minute Disappearing Act—have a "Sense Of Accomplishment Reaction." You'll SOAR after you have completed a necessary task early on.

That email you meant to reply to but kept putting off? Write it, hit the send button, and you'll SOAR. That small but noticeable rush of self-satisfaction for completing that pesky task is the perfect way to start the day. During your 20-Minute Disappearing Act, complete one task like that, whether it has a high or low priority on your list of things to do. When you cross it off your list, you'll achieve a more positive state of mind. You'll have a better feeling about yourself and your day, and the remaining tasks will almost certainly be addressed with a higher level of confidence and enthusiasm.

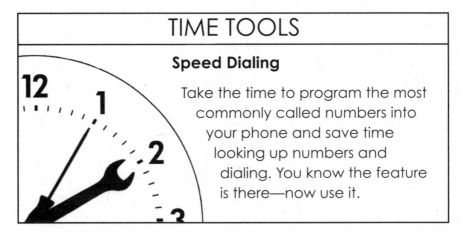

TIME TOOLS

Speed Dialing

Take the time to program the most commonly called numbers into your phone and save time looking up numbers and dialing. You know the feature is there—now use it.

The rush of satisfaction (SOARing) that people feel when they accomplish a goal may have its roots in a chemical reaction in the human brain.

A group of neurotransmitters, called endorphins, affect a person's mood, among other things. Many of the intense positive feelings experienced by humans as a reaction to outside stimuli are related to endorphin release. Endorphins allow people to feel a sense of power and control over themselves. Although there is no medical evidence yet, people report feeling a strong "rush" of exhilaration when they complete a goal, similar to the rush one receives from the influence of endorphin release.

Conventional time management principles encourage businesspeople to tackle the highest-priority tasks first. But we believe reinforcing a positive sense of accomplishment in the first 20 minutes is an important first step to getting the entire day's work under control.

Maybe you'll decide to set up an appointment, prepare an outline, or make a quick phone call as the task that gets you to SOAR. Whatever it is, don't let it take more than five to seven minutes of your 20-Minute Disappearing Act. You need time to think and organize while you're still invisible. If you spend the whole 20 minutes on small tasks, you won't have a plan of action for the day.

Using a Timer

A timer is useful not only during your 20-Minute Disappearing Act, but also throughout the day, as you work on your various responsibilities. Timeboxing, a technique used by software developers, refers to creating a fixed deadline. You will accomplish the most valuable work possible during the limited time that's available. When you work within the time limit you have set, you:

◆ Stop procrastinating. When you have an ominous project looming overhead, getting started can be the most critical and most challenging part. Try setting your timer for just 20 minutes, and do as much as you can in that time. When the timer rings, you may want to keep working, or you may need to restart tomorrow for another 20 minutes. The important thing is, you've gotten started.

◆ Use time efficiently. When a timer limits your time, even artificially, you focus more clearly on the task in front of you. You feel a sense of urgency, which helps you automatically prioritize and complete the parts of the task that are truly worthwhile.

◆ Get the job done. Setting a timer can keep you on track in each of your projects. But when you are confronted with a deadline and are required to finish a task, you may need to give it preference over the rest of your schedule. If you start working on a task as soon as it is assigned, you can painlessly chip away at it just by writing it into your schedule—an hour here, a half-hour here, and so on.

31

Timing is Everything

The final challenge of the 20-Minute Disappearing Act: get it done in 20 minutes! In the worst-case scenario, your first activity runs so long that it upsets the timing of the rest of your day. Oh, the irony! Practice the 20-Minute Disappearing Act as a management discipline. Set an egg timer, your alarm watch, or your computer. We can't forget there's a business to run and people who need you who are lined up right outside your door.

Seeing the Big Picture

An invaluable advantage of your 20-Minute Disappearing Act is the shift in perspective it provides. Taking a breath at the beginning of the day allows you to see the big picture, instead of immediately getting engrossed in all the details of everyday work. We all want to think the work we do is important, but when we get bogged down in the weeds, we can't always take the time to smell the roses.

Keeping those long-term goals in mind each day during the 20-Minute Disappearing Act is a good way to remind yourself that you have a long-range strategy. Each small task may not always be the most exciting part of the job, but if the task helps you build to a predetermined goal, then the small tasks become more meaningful and satisfying, and less annoying or onerous.

With that schedule for the day in hand, you're ready to reappear and get started!

> " If you want to make good use of your time, you've got to know what's most important and then give it all you've got."
>
> – Lee Iacocca, former CEO, Chrysler Corporation

Back to Alex...

Monday morning, two weeks later. Alex arrives at 9:17 a.m. To outmaneuver the piranhas, he enters the restaurant through the receiving door, inspecting the compactor area along the way. He stealthily slips into his office and shuts the door. He sets the timer on his computer for 20 minutes. Twenty minutes of uninterrupted peace. It is probably the quietest time he will have all day. He brings up his to-do list on his computer and sees an item about a setting up an appointment with his wholesaler. Alex writes a quick email and hits "Send." Already, he's SOARing! Then Alex reviews his schedule for the rest of the day. He checks the rest of his to-do list, sorts through his "Today" file, then leans back and tries to visualize the tasks that lie ahead.

The timer rings, and Alex has his plan for the day in hand. He steps out of his office and rallies the staff together. He now realizes that when he is in control, his staff doesn't seem like a group of raging piranhas, but more like a school of motivated fish.

Summary of Chapter Three:

During the first few minutes of your workday, you establish your pace, your posture, and your productivity level. If you want to be calm, confident, and constructive for the rest of the day, then perform your 20-Minute Disappearing Act as soon as your workday begins.

How to Use Your First 20 Minutes:

1. Check your calendar for fixed appointments, meetings, and upcoming deadlines.

2. Review your goals for the week and near term.

3. Use those goals to refine and clarify the to-do list you started yesterday, deciding which tasks are unnecessary, of minor importance, of high importance, and essential.

4. Contact the people you need to assist you in achieving your goals

early in the day. You'll have a better chance of connecting.

5. SOAR—enjoy the endorphin rush early in the day.

6. Plan out most of the rest of your day, blocking out time for fixed and flexible responsibilities, giving higher priorities preference.

TIMELESS ADVICE

Writer Samuel Butler said, "If you follow reason far enough it always leads to conclusions that are contrary to reason." This statement really applies to the 20-Minute Disappearing Act. Twenty minutes of thoughtful planning early in your day will yield a far more productive workday.

CHAPTER 4

ZAP!
The Distractions

*"You can always find a distraction
if you're looking for one."*
– Tom Kite, professional golfer

*L*ogan is thrilled to move into her first real four-walled office. For nearly two years she's been in the "open pit" cubicle area at the company, and was longing for some needed privacy to concentrate. Now, with her promotion in hand and walls and door around her, she is ready to become the most productive department manager ever.

Just one problem. Her brand-new private office is rather unfortunately located right next to the reception area. A constant parade of people marches past her door. With the door open, everyone looks in and has something to discuss. With the door closed, she can hear what's happening just outside the office and then feels she is missing out on things. She hears the receptionist's phone ring. She hears deliveries coming in. She knows who is visiting anyone on her floor. Somehow, the private office is even more distracting than the open cubicles!

"I don't understand why I can't get more work done," Logan thinks. "But everything seems to distract me." Logan knows it is important to be accessible to her staff whenever they need her—after all, she is the boss now, and has the final say when they have issues to resolve. Their never-ending

*email messages demand her immediate response, and if people aren't phys-
ically in her office, they are on the phone.*

*Customers, associates, and other managers can easily get her away from
what she is doing, just to ask her a "quick question," the answer to which
is usually guaranteed to turn into a 15-minute chat. At the end of the
day, Logan feels that she has not accomplished much of anything. "I'm
being pulled in too many directions all day long," she thinks, "without
being able to focus."*

Sources of Distractions

Now that you've performed your 20-Minute Disappearing Act, the vital
first step in a time-managed day, you're ready to jump into the thick of
things. A study by Basex in 2006 showed that the average worker is distracted off the task at hand every 11 minutes. Once interrupted, it takes
anywhere from two to twenty-five minutes to get your mind back on
track to the original task. How can anyone get things done with such a
steady stream of distractions? Truthfully, it's next to impossible. More
must be done to ZAP! at least some of the countless distractions that
confront us every day.

Here is a list of six major sources of distractions in most workplaces.
Your workplace may have somewhat different ones from those on this
list. But most people recognize these six distractions as the top offenders when it comes to keeping us from the task at hand.

Stop Throwing Time Away!

A study by Salary.com in 2006 found that interruptions cost the average worker 2 hours out of
every 8-hour day. That's 25% of your workday
wasted. One-quarter! Employers spend $544 bil-
lion per year on salaries for which real work is expected, but none is done.

1. Paperwork

2. Email

3. Noise

4. Staff

5. Telephones

6. Internet surfing for personal use

We'll deal with each of these sources of distraction and suggest ways to ZAP! them from your work environment. Some of them are simple; others require a major investment of time in order to yield positive results. It is important to take the time to get your distractions under control before they start to negatively impact your working day.

Dealing with Paperwork

A practice commonly espoused by time management experts is never to handle a piece of paper more than once. But many people find this nearly impossible to do. Try thinking of paperwork a different way: all paper should be handled as if it were treated with a radioactive substance or typed with radioactive ink. With this in mind, you'll realize that the more times you handle a particular piece of paper, the more likely you are to get "sick" of it.

If you can handle a particular piece of paper only once, that's best. But if you think of paper as radioactive, work to minimize your exposure to each piece of paperwork on your desk. The 4-D Rule can help: Do It, Dump It, Defer It, or Delegate It. The emphasis should be on the Do It option, but closely behind in second place is to Dump It. If you can find a way to dump the work, then do so. Then it can't possibly return at a later date to rob you of your time. Put a trashcan beside your desk and use it.

Sometimes, making the choice to Defer It may be the most time-effective option, depending on the issue and how much time you have at

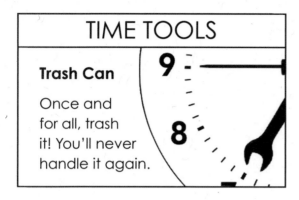

TIME TOOLS

Trash Can

Once and for all, trash it! You'll never handle it again.

that moment to attend to it. But be careful where you put the paper once you have decided to Defer It. Losing or misplacing it can rob you of hours each week. One technique that works well for handling paperwork is to use a two-drawer file cabinet. If you don't have an office, use two large accordion-type files that you keep in the trunk of your car.

Divide drawer one into sections and label each section with titles that make sense for your job. An office manager like our friend Logan might use categories such as these:

- Business Development Ideas
- Cost Control
- Customer Relations
- Delegated Tasks
- Employee Development
- Employee Meeting Topics
- Employee Recruiting
- Form Letters
- Insurance
- Management Development
- Office Equipment Service
- On-Line Operations
- Operations Checklist
- Performance Reviews
- Personal Development
- Safety Committee

If you're not ready to act on the issue addressed by a specific piece of mail and you don't want to dump it, deferring it to one of these files is the most efficient alternative. A study conducted by AccounTemps, a company that places temporary accountants, showed that executives spent 4.3 hours a week looking for items that were mislabeled, misfiled, or misplaced. You can do better. A filing system for paperwork based on categories that make sense for your job will help you put your hands on the paper when it's time to deal with it.

The second drawer or file box should be slotted and numbered from 1 to 31. Each file number represents a day of the month. If you know what day is the right one to deal with the paperwork, and it's not today, file the item in the day that's best. It's a good idea to check the file slot for the day you're planning during your 20-Minute Disappearing Act. No more rummaging around in a sea of paper trying to find a letter you received 10 days ago but need now. Manage your mail and paperwork so it can't ZAP! the energy you'll need to handle the remaining distractions.

Finally, Delegate It. Quickly determine if the paperwork can be dealt with by someone else and pass it along. That's it. Delegating is key to managing your time, so we've devoted a whole chapter to improving your abilities in this area (Chapter 6).

Dealing with Email

Email—can't live without it, but can't live with it, either. It's a great tool for quick communication, but for many businesspeople, email can take

> " I use my credenzas and bookshelves to organize my work and paperwork. The only thing on my desk is the one project I am working on at the time and my computer. If I really need to focus on the project, I will close the computer screen so the project in front of me gets undivided and special attention."
>
> – Dan Butler, VP, Retail Operations, National Retail Federation

over your workday. Email is like regular mail, only more so. The ease in sending email has made the volume of email grow exponentially. Few businesspeople received 75 letters a day when all we had was snail mail. But it's not unusual to have 75 or more important email messages waiting in your in-box every morning.

TIME TOOLS

Two In-Baskets

A great tool to help expedite the Defer It process is the common in-basket. Use two in-baskets stacked on the corner of your desk. Label the top basket "ETD"—Empty This Day. Label the bottom basket "ETW"—Empty This Week. During your 20-Minute Disappearing Act at the start of the day or in your last ten minutes of the day, stash the materials that don't belong in the topics file or the 1–31 file in either the ETD basket, if it has to be executed that day, or the ETW basket, if it absolutely, positively has to be dealt with by the end of the week.

You won't lose time looking for that letter you had to respond to by 4:00 p.m. today, or that agenda you had to complete by 5:00 p.m. Friday. And what a satisfying feeling it is to leave your work space at the end of the day eyeing that emptied ETD basket. Or when the last moments of your week roll around and there's nothing in that vacated ETW basket.

There are a few issues about email that help to make it a giant time-waster. The first is the sheer volume. Start with the best spam filter you can get, so that most email you really don't want to read will go to your junk folder. Once a day, scan your junk folder to be sure something important didn't get in there that you want to see. Then hit "Delete All."

You'll still get plenty of email, even when your spam filter is vigilant. Because it is so easy, people tend to cc everyone in the organization, when in reality, only a few people really need to receive the message. You can try to reduce this by being a good example. Don't send cc's unnecessarily, and feel free to tell people, especially those who report to you, when and how to decide if you need to be cc'd on their email messages.

To keep email from eating up your valuable time, we recommend you check your email on a scheduled basis—maybe at the start of your day (NOT during your 20-Minute Disappearing Act), before lunch, after lunch, and before you leave for the day. This is a hard discipline to maintain. Some people expect that you will respond to email instantaneously, and if your boss is one of those people, you may have to check more often. But like dealing with paperwork, handling email in a group is a much more efficient way to use your time. Let people know you don't immediately respond to email so they aren't offended if your reply isn't instantaneous.

> " There are managers so preoccupied with their e-mail messages that they never look up from their screens to see what's happening in the nondigital world."
>
> – *Mihaly Csikszentmihalyi, Professor of Psychology and Management, The Drucker School, Claremont Graduate University*

Turn off the "ping"! Most people just can't ignore that sound that says, "Somebody out there wants to communicate with me!" Don't let new email drive your workflow—your priorities should be in charge. Change your computer's settings to make no sound when a new email comes in, and check email on *your* schedule. Deal with email messages in the order in which they arrived.

If you are someone who can't resist the little number on your mail program icon that tells you how many new messages are there, get rid of that feature, too. Just change your settings in mail preferences to "Check for new mail manually" rather than any automatic alternative. You'll have to hit the "get mail" button that retrieves mail when you want it—kind of like walking down to the mailbox to see what the postman brought in days of old! Now *you* are in charge of when you choose to get your email, instead of senders being able to distract you nonstop.

Another email time-waster can be scrolling through the inbox filled with old messages, looking for some information that was sent to you earlier. It's just like dealing with the paper mail—if you haven't filed it in the appropriate slot when you decided to Defer It, it's nearly impossible to find it when you want it. Establish a system of filing email messages you want to keep to refer to later, or your email in-box will be a long list of messages that will take too much time to read through when you're looking for one message in particular.

Handle email the way you handle paperwork: the 4-D system again. You'll have to read through each email in your in-box. But here's the important part. Do something with each email as soon as you read it. If it is a Do It item, reply right away. Then trash the email or file it if you need to refer to it later. Then on to the next email. If it's a Dump It email, trash it right away. If it's a Defer It, then use those email files or save the message and place it in an appropriate file on your computer. If you want to Delegate It, forward the email immediately to the right person with a short note explaining how to handle it.

You get the idea. Deal with all email as you read them, one by one. When you get to the end of your in-box, you should have every email handled and the inbox should be clear.

Dealing with Noise

A study of noise distraction in the workplace revealed the following comments:

> "I made simple programming mistakes that cost hours of debugging."

> "Inspirations would disappear into thin air and never return."

> "When you have to keep twenty things in your head at one time, you can't afford to be overhearing your co-worker's phone calls."

Seventy percent of office workers say they would be more productive with a reduction in noise. And the kind of noise that is most distracting in the office is human speech.

There are a few ways to deal with distracting noise. If you have a private office, you can try a white noise machine. It generates a background "buzz" that effectively wipes out most other kinds of noises. A bubbling water garden or an electric fan also create this kind of white noise.

In some situations, headphones can be a great way to tune out noise distraction. If you can work with soothing background music, headphones set at a low volume are the answer. Plus, when people see that you are wearing headphones, they are less likely to start up idle conversations. If they try, you can point to your ears and smile. Most likely, they'll get the message and go away.

Dealing with Staff/Visitors

Logan's in a tough position—being next to the reception area means everyone coming and going peeks in her office and stops to chat. She doesn't want to be seen as unfriendly, and of course, she wants to maintain an open door policy with her staff. But that open door seems like an open invitation to everyone in the office.

Take a tip from college professors. They schedule office hours to let students know that during those times, they are available in their office for questions, comments, and help—whatever the students want to discuss. They are often in their offices other times, too, but students know that the posted office hours are specifically reserved for them. Try this with your staff. Set aside a block of time each day that are your open office hours. Make it clear that these times are for your staff, and that you want them to make use of these hours if they have a question or need to discuss a project. Naturally, you're in your office plenty of other times during the day, but everyone will know that they will have your undivided attention during the posted hours.

If your job requires receiving visits from vendors and salespeople, you have an additional source of visitor distraction. Vendors will take advantage of a lackadaisical time manager. If you are known to accept visitors at any time of the day, salespeople will use you to fill the voids in their day. You, in effect, will be working their schedule, not yours. Have open office hours for sales reps and vendors, and stick to them.

How do you politely tell someone he or she is interrupting you? Your office door, if you have one, is a great time management tool that should be utilized. A fully open door suggests that anyone can come in at any time. A door just cracked open an inch or two signals, "I'm here, but I'm busy doing something." In other words, "If it can wait, it should." A closed door clearly communicates that you are too busy for any interruption, except, of course, an emergency situation. These three positions and their meanings can be easily explained in a staff meeting.

Another approach that can work whether or not you have a door is to use actual signs. These signs can be attached to the office door or stuck on the wall beside your cubicle entry. The idea behind each sign is to communicate a message that you're willing—or not—to be interrupted. You can be humorous or very direct. In any event, the message will be clear: you are in control of your working/thinking area!

One Ohio retailer sends an effective, silent time management message to his staff. When he arrives at work, he leaves his coat on as he begins his day in the office or on the sales floor. Everyone knows not to approach him until his coat comes off! In effect, his coat serves as a time

ENTER HERE

I'm certain what you have to say will contribute greatly to my day.

YIELD

Please be sure this visit is important.

STOP

Please do not interrupt. Serious work in progress.

management tool. If you don't have an office or a door, this idea may work for you.

Once inside your office, the arrangement of your furniture can dramatically impact the number of interruptions you experience. Never position your desk so it faces the door or your office mate's desk. It's second nature to look up as someone passes your office if your desk faces right out to the hallway. Even if you don't want to be distracted, you'll find yourself doing this if your sight lines make it easy. Position your desk at an angle that faces a wall. In this position, the hallway distractions are limited to your peripheral vision and you'll find yourself stopping to check out the person going by much less often. We don't advise arranging your furniture so your back is to everyone who enters your office. Practitioners of Feng Shui design would say that your back to the door disrupts the flow of the energy. It may send a harsher signal to your workmates than you would like.

Here's another good habit to develop. If someone ZAPS! you unexpectedly with a distraction, say something like, "I can't talk right this second, but I want to see you as soon as possible." Agree on a specific date, time, and place when this person's issue can be addressed, instead of interrupting your schedule. Immediately record it on your notepad or to-do list. This practice is especially important if the person who needs an answer is an employee. Your eagerness to deal with questions or problems will be noticed and appreciated. You will appear empathetic and responsive. Most importantly, you will be treating an employee with respect. And you will have slotted the distraction where it can be handled in a planned, organized manner. You are back in control!

Dealing with the Telephone

One of the most potent distractions that can ZAP! you is the telephone. With a simple ring, your focused brain is sent whirling like a shake machine: "I wonder who's calling me now. It better not be that so-and-so." And if it is a wrong number or misdirected call? You have just been mentally derailed. You have lost your focus. And it may be several minutes before you're back on track.

Whether or not you have a private office, there are several ways you can minimize distractions from the telephone. Start by changing the phone itself—put a 20-foot cord on your handset, use a speakerphone, or change to a portable handset or a wearable headset. All of these options will give you more freedom to move, and you can choose the one that works best for your work environment. If the call is a necessary interruption, you can remain mobile enough to move about the office and multi-task simultaneously.

If you have some authority over an open office environment, we strongly recommend changing the ringer to a light on all the phones. This way, the other phones' ringers won't distract you or anyone else. If you can't make that change, turn the volume of the ringers down. Again, you will minimize neighboring distractions for everyone.

Use your message to avoid wasting time on phone interruptions. Don't be afraid to let the machine get it. In your message, ask the incoming caller to prioritize the importance of his or her call. It sounds harsh, but it works. Here is a sample message for your answering machine to repeat: "I'm not available to take your call right now. Please leave your name and your message. Would you please also indicate the urgency of your call? If it is urgent, say Priority One; if it is a call I can return tomorrow, use Priority Two; and if I can call you within the next three to five days, that would be a Priority Three. For example, 'Herb, this is Carlos. Please call me at ###-####, Priority Two.' Thank you."

People who know you're a time manager will be willing to cooperate. First-time callers may be initially surprised by this system but will quickly learn you're serious about your time and this time management technique. And of course, you have to return the call when you say you will. Otherwise, no one will use your system again.

Dealing with Internet Surfing

Polls show that the biggest distraction for people at work is their own personal Internet use. That may seem strange—all the other distractions we've talked about are imposed on a person from the outside. But no one makes you surf the Internet for your own personal use. It just seems to be a temptation many people cannot avoid.

If you're someone who clicks on a news page every few minutes to see the latest goings-on in the world, or checks a sports website to follow your favorite team, or watches the progress of eBay auctions while at work, you need some tips on how to keep the Internet surfing to a minimum. Many businesspeople spend all day sitting in front of a computer, and often they are using the Internet as part of a work task. It can be hard NOT to zip over to a personal site when the work gets a little boring or your mind wanders.

Keep the temptation of the Internet away as much as possible. It will require some willpower on your part. Start by keeping the Internet turned off unless you are actively using it for work. When

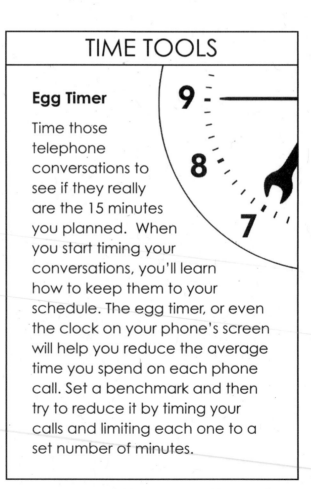

TIME TOOLS

Egg Timer

Time those telephone conversations to see if they really are the 15 minutes you planned. When you start timing your conversations, you'll learn how to keep them to your schedule. The egg timer, or even the clock on your phone's screen will help you reduce the average time you spend on each phone call. Set a benchmark and then try to reduce it by timing your calls and limiting each one to a set number of minutes.

> " When I'm working on a project or writing an article, I don't check email. If the phone rings, I let it go to voice mail. I lock my office door and put up a Post-It note that says, 'Writing Troll—Get Back!' which has a picture of a troll on it. The troll is a warning. They know if they bypass the troll, they'll be confronted by an ogre."
>
> *– Steve Pavlina, personal development blogger*

you're done with a work task that requires using the Internet, close your web browser.

If you use Facebook, MySpace, Twitter, or any other social media sites on a regular basis, you know how much time you can waste chatting. Make it a practice to visit those social media sites only during non-work hours. Think of them as friends you visit after work.

The same practice should hold for instant messenger sites. Turn them off at work. You don't need your friends instant messaging you all day and expecting you to chat online while you're working. Save that for home.

Set your bookmarks on your web browser for sites related to work only. If you can't get to your favorite time-intensive sites with just one click, there's less chance you'll click to them when you want distraction.

There are applications on the web to help you tame the digital distractions. Some simply monitor what you do on the web to give you insight into your daily surfing habits. If you know how much you are distracted, you know what to avoid. You'll get a sense of how much time you spend on various Internet websites, as well as on software programs, emailing, social networks, and other places you go to regularly.

Other software can actually stop you from using programs you want to avoid at work by blocking them at your request. This can be helpful to keep you away from digital distractions that you know are especially powerful.

We all know how entertaining our computers can be, especially when we are looking for a way to procrastinate or distract ourselves while on the job. Don't let this machine take over your time. It's a tool, like many others you use at work. Take control of your computer and you'll take more control over your time.

IT'S TRUE

In 2007, Intel experimented with quiet time for 300 engineers. For seven months, the engineers made four contiguous hours each week quiet ones by sending phone calls to voice mail, putting up Do Not Disturb signs, avoiding meetings, and working offline. The goal was to give the engineers concentrated time to think. The company found that some employees used their quiet time for creative projects, while others found the breathing space was important for gaining control over their day.

(Source: The *Conference Board Review*, Nov./Dec. 2008)

Logan, Part Deux:

After a few weeks of feeling like every person in the company visited her new office 20 times a day, Logan made some strategic changes to her space.

She started by rearranging her office furniture. Instead of sitting with her desk facing the office door, she repositioned it to face a wall, where she hung a bulletin board with a large calendar on it. She put a large schefflera plant beside her desk to shield her from people who peek in to see if she's not busy. She bought a white noise machine and enjoys its comforting hum that muffles the sound of the receptionist nearby. Logan moved the two-drawer file from the corner of the office to the immediate right of her desk and set up a system for filing Defer It papers.

Now Logan's phone calls are set to go straight to voice mail, and she reviews the messages hourly, making sure to handle crises immediately, and everything else as needed. She reset some of her computer settings to make her less liable to distract herself with Internet surfing, even going so far as to take off her favorite shopping sites.

Logan finds that she has more time to deal with customers and staff when she arranges to see them on HER schedule, not on everyone else's. She recognizes that she has more time and gets more done every day. She knows that keeping distractions at bay is partly responsible for these newly discovered minutes.

Summary of Chapter Four:

Distractions abound in the workplace. It's hard to maintain your work flow when people are stopping by to chat, telephones are ringing all over, your email keeps beeping, and the Internet is omnipresent. Change what you can in your environment to minimize the distractions all around you, and you'll find that you're in much more control over your time and your work.

How to ZAP! the Distractions:

1. Rearrange your office furniture to avoid looking directly at passersby.

2. Get rid of the email "ping" and check email only at scheduled intervals.

3. Send your telephone calls to voice mail as much as possible and return them in batches.

4. Keep your web browser turned off except when using it for work-related tasks.

5. Use your door and signs to signal others for the right time to "pop in."

TIMELESS ADVICE

Remember Newton's First Law? "A body in motion tends to stay in motion unless acted upon by an outside force." The laws of nature are on your side. It's the outside distractions that are working against you. Minimize these outside forces to keep your body in motion and to maximize your momentum.

CHAPTER 5

Make the To-Do List!

*"One of the secrets of getting more done
is to make a to do list every day,
keep it visible, and use it as a guide to action
as you go through the day."*
– Jean de la Fontaine, French Poet

*L*ogan stops by Starbucks after a particularly exhausting day at work. "An iced mocha latte," she thinks, "will be a great pick-me-up on my way home." When she walks back to her car, she starts fishing for her keys that are buried at the bottom of her huge handbag/briefcase. She takes out her large leather-bound planner and sets it on the roof of the car while looking. And we all know what happens next: she finds the keys, hops into the car, bag in one hand, keys and latte in the other, and zooms off…with the planner flying off the roof.

Logan is nearly hysterical when she realizes the planner is gone. She's a self-proclaimed "to-do list fanatic," and the loss of her future's blueprint sends her over the edge (not to mention the triple espresso shots in that iced latte). "How am I going to remember everything I've written in my planner?" she wails.

Her planner was full of to-do's written on scrap paper and clipped to the planner's pages.

Logan is distraught. "All the details, all the activities, all the appointments—I'll never be able to reconstruct them, and no one else has that information!"

To-Do Today Lists Are Essential

There is no way around it. Typed, handwritten, or computer-generated To-Do Today lists are essential in business. What you need to do today must be outlined in advance, whether you use a paper notebook, an electronic planner, or you tape-record your list.

People who perform this daily ritual on a regular basis are far more productive than those who do not. These To-Doers are good time managers. They know what they need to do and can prioritize the tasks that are needed to achieve those goals. To-Doers allocate the appropriate amount of time to each task, and make the most of each day. They contact the people they need to help execute their plans in advance, thereby increasing the odds that those tasks will be completed, because the resource person they need will be available. And To-Doers look back at the end of each workday to evaluate how effective they were at completing what was on the list. They take pride in their accomplishments, understand what didn't go as planned, and are better prepared to redirect a new attack on the problem the next day.

Why Most Managers Don't Make To-Do Today Lists

The To-Do Today list is one of the most basic tools in our time management tool chest. But only twenty percent of business people draft a thorough to-do list most of the time. Why do most people in business ignore the list?

> ❝ Before you do anything, make a list of what's important to you. If the list is longer than six things, shorten it. Don't work on much else until you've finished something on your list.”
>
> – Danny Wegman, CEO, Wegmans Food Markets, Inc.

Some of the most frequent responses to this question include:

- ◆ "I don't have enough personal control over my day to do a good job planning it."

- ◆ "I never seem to get the list completed, so why bother?"

- ◆ "It's frustrating to see that my list keeps growing."

- ◆ "I don't really know how to make a good to-do list."

- ◆ "I don't have time to make a list."

Let's analyze each of these common reasons why generally intelligent, well-meaning managers shy away from making the to-do list.

1. "I don't have enough personal control over my day to do a good job planning it."

This number one response is a classic self-fulfilling prophecy. When you believe that you have little or no control over your work, you'll soon discover that you don't. Drop the negative attitude! You will find all aspects of your life, both work and personal, to be far more enjoyable when you regain a leadership role in your own life. Look for opportunities to regain control over your activities at work by making a To-Do Today list and sticking by it.

Believe it or not, you have a lot of say over how you spend your time. While it's true that customers, bosses, and people in positions of authority at work have the power to influence your schedule, ultimately, you are in charge. The sooner you recognize this fact, the sooner you'll be on the way to taking charge of your own time and making each day more productive.

Accept the few occasions when you must defer to the demands of others. For the most part, set the pace of your own life by starting with setting your daily schedule. If you change your attitude to, "I can control more of my life than I previously imagined," then you're on your way to a more organized and productive work life.

2. "I never seem to get the list done, so why bother?"

First, who ever said the entire To-Do Today list has to be completed? Some managers keep a running to-do list that never ends. New projects are simply added to an existing list and those completed tasks are crossed off. Don't be so hard on yourself. When the list you have drafted early in the day remains largely untouched due to unexplained events, think about why those unplanned events occurred. Determine if you could identify them the next time they crop up. Then, rewrite your next day's To-Do Today list starting with those incomplete assignments from the day before. Good news—tomorrow will greet you with 24 more hours!

Second, allow for some flexibility in your plan. One effective manager we know plans only 45 minutes of each hour, allowing 15 minutes for the unplanned events—those "list busters." It's a good idea to leave empty spaces at the bottom of your to-do list for unplanned events that arise. The degree to which your job involves outside interaction will dictate the amount of flex-time you need to build into your list.

> " Besides the noble art of getting things done, there is the noble art of leaving things undone. The wisdom of life consists of the elimination of non-essentials."
>
> *– Lyn Yatang, Chinese writer* '

Go easy on yourself while learning to use a To-Do Today list. The more confidence you develop and the more positive attitude you adopt regarding your list, the more likely you will continue to use this tool.

3. "It's frustrating to see that my list keeps growing."

Congratulations! Your job sounds secure! In a world of downsizing, someone is generally left with all the things spun off by others, and that's you. If your To-Do Today list keeps growing, great—you'll be employed— but you must become a master of prioritizing and delegating. You'll see items disappear from your list as you find more ways to get them accomplished.

4. "I don't really know how to make a good to-do list."

To-Do Today lists can, and should, be the simplest of time management tools. Anyone can make a useful To-Do Today list because they should be kept as streamlined as possible. There are plenty of to-do list templates available on the Internet and elsewhere, but they generally boil down to two simple elements—*what* needs to be done and its *priority.*

5. "I don't have time to make a To-Do Today list."

Huh? Are you serious? Think about it.

Creating the To-Do Today List

Since it is so important for managing time, we'll help you understand the basics of how to create a useful list, and how to make sure To-Doing becomes part of your daily routine. It is a simple tool, but there are plenty of tricks to making the To-Do Today list more effective.

Do Your Laundry First

A simple two-step process is a great way to create an effective, usable To-Do Today list for most business people. Start with a laundry list of all the tasks you want to accomplish. Note the task, its priority, and if possible, categorize it broadly according to its type of work. Retailers, for example, may find four categories are descriptive of most of the work they do: "Sales Building," "Cost Reduction," "Margin Enhancement," and "Associates Development." Someone managing a clothing store will spend most time on items that involve making sales, controlling costs, managing the cost of goods, and developing staff. Someone who works as a supervisor in a manufacturing company will have other categories: perhaps "Production," "Associates Development," and "Cost Control." Whatever you do, start by determining the major categories of work that are most important to your job. Then assign your tasks for the day into one of those categories on the To-Do Worksheet. Anything else gets thrown in an "Other" category.

Set Your Priorities

For each task, categorize it and then decide its priority. How important is it to you or your boss that the task is completed? Use a simple rating system for assessing priorities. A "1" means top priority—it has to be accomplished right away. A "4" is for a task that can wait. It must be something that has to get done, or it wouldn't be on your list at all, but it's not a pressing item for that day. "2" and "3" are in between, of course.

Although some tasks can be handled concurrently, most have to be dealt with one at a time. On quick evaluation, it is easy to determine that one task seems more important than the rest, and so on. You'll work on the tasks on your list in priority order. Then, if you are forced to abandon your plan because something new had to take precedence, you can take comfort in the fact that you have already tackled and accomplished the top 1 or 2 goals that you had planned for that day.

Polish the List

Step two of creating a To-Do Today list is rewriting the worksheet into a more polished To-Do Today list, complete with two more headings: *who* will do the task, and the *due date* for completion of each task. When you have this, you have a To-Do Today list that you can really use!

Group the activities on your laundry list by category. Put the priority 1 items at the top of each category, and work down from there. Now spend a few more minutes deciding on the *who* and the *when* for each task.

To-Do Worksheet

		Code	Priority
1.	Meet with night crew about damages	C	1
2.	~~Discuss ad campaign with managers~~	S	2
3.	Steve's performance review	A	1
4.	Pick up stamps at post office	O	3
5.			
6.			
7.			
8.			
9.			
10.			
11.			
12.			
13.			
14.			

(S) = Sales Building   (C) = Cost Reduction   (M) = Margin Enhancement
(A) = Associate Development   (O) = Other

Priority   1 = Highest   4=Lowest

Laundry List of Tasks

To whom can you delegate each task? If you're a manager or supervisor, these assignments should be very easy to make. But even if you don't have any staff for whom you're responsible, there are often other people who are best to take a task on your list. Maybe one of your items is to buy stamps for the office, and the task pops up on your to-do list more often than you'd like. Is there someone else in the office who can do this task? There may be a delivery person who is driving around town as part of his or her job and can easily add a stop at the post office to his or her to-do list. Or maybe you can automate this task by buying stamps at regular intervals or installing a postage meter.

Once you've determined who will handle each task (and many of them are still going to be you, in all likelihood), set a due date for each one. Number 1 priorities will probably have to be completed by the end of the day. You may need to set a specific time, too. Number 4s may have a date that is a week away.

After this process is complete, look carefully at the activities labeled "Other." Analyze the amount of time allocated to activities that don't have a direct correlation to your major business building categories. Then answer this question: "Why do it?" Too often business people find themselves immersed in trivial, noncritical tasks that eventually become bad habits. For example, many supervisors complain about not having time to do regular employee evaluations, but seem to find time to open all the mail every day, even the junk mail! This is a simple task that a lower-level (and lower paid) employee could perform. Do you want to avoid the important tasks in favor of items that are simple? That's not the mind-set of a time manager.

> " Never tell people how to do things.
> Tell them what to do and they will
> surprise you with their ingenuity."
> – George S. Patton, Jr., General, U.S. Army

Sales Builder	Delegate To	Due Date
_____	_____	_____
_____	_____	_____
_____	_____	_____

Cost Control	Delegate To	Due Date
_____	_____	_____
_____	_____	_____
_____	_____	_____

Margin Enhancement	Delegate To	Due Date
_____	_____	_____
_____	_____	_____
_____	_____	_____

Associate Development	Delegate To	Due Date
_____	_____	_____
_____	_____	_____
_____	_____	_____

Other	Delegate To	Due Date
_____	_____	_____
_____	_____	_____
_____	_____	_____

To-Do Today List

One of your aims should be to eliminate the "Other" category. On the sample to-do list on page 61 there is a dotted line above the "Other" category. We suggest you take a pair of scissors to it—zip this strip and toss it! In most cases, your work revolves around the main categories you have established, and you don't need to waste time with activities that do not involve them. From time to time, you will have an important task on your To-Do Today list that doesn't directly fit in your major categories. Maybe you need to attend a Lion's Club luncheon or a Chamber of Commerce function. You can certainly justify the time allocated to these duties. But if "Other" items seem to consume more

IT'S TRUE !

Over 40 years ago, Charles E. Hummel wrote a small booklet titled *Tyranny of the Urgent*. In it, he talked about the need to set priorities. His ideas have been echoed by time and life managers ever since. He sets up the problem that we all encounter:

"Have you ever wished for a thirty-hour day? Surely some extra time would relieve the tremendous pressure under which we live."

Hummel recognized that more time isn't the answer. The problem to conquer is how to set priorities carefully and adhere to them. He encouraged people to determine what was really important, and not let tasks that are urgent "crowd out the important" from our lives.

time than any other category on your To-Do Today list, it is time to analyze your schedule. An overloaded "Other" category is a sure sign that a businessperson's priorities are skewed and he or she has lost focus.

Puncture a Project

When a project is large, many people have a tendency to put it off, even if the task isn't objectionable. Remember when you were a child and were told to clean your room? You would say, "The whole room? That's so much to do!" But if Mom was clever enough to say first, "make the bed," and then say, "put the toys away," what seemed like a huge task wasn't so tough after all.

When developing the to-do list, break down the tasks into small pieces. We call this "puncturing" the project—dissecting any major to-do item into logical, reasonable component parts. Then, as your schedule permits, set out to perform one of the component parts at a time. After several days or weeks you will see that the task that at first seemed insurmountable is now only a fragment of its former self. You have effectively punctured holes in the project and completed it over time, piece by piece.

> " A cinch by the inch,
> but hard by the yard."
>
> – Old Adage

Look at each major to-do item on your list as if you were writing a new book. The task of writing 200 pages of original, creative, and interesting text may seem impossible. But using the concept of puncturing the project, you can start with the task of developing the overall concept for the book. Then each chapter can be addressed one at a time. You can puncture the project further by breaking down each chapter into component parts. Peck away at each chapter and eventually the book is written.

Use this same idea to break down your large projects into manageable tasks. If a task you write on your To-Do Today list seems daunting and you put it off because it's overwhelming, then puncture the project. Break it down into smaller parts. Determine the steps needed to get the whole task done and write those steps on your To-Do Today list. Then they can be tackled on *your* schedule. Prioritize them, polish them, and delegate them when possible, and sure enough, you'll see that major project completed in due time.

Draft Your Laundry List

At the end of your workday, make your laundry list of all the tasks that you think want to accomplish tomorrow. Writing the laundry list at the end of the day helps to ensure that all the activities that need attention tomorrow are recorded while they are still fresh in your mind. Break down the items into manageable parts and put on only the tasks you think you can accomplish tomorrow. Set other parts of that item aside for another To-Do Today list.

TIME TOOLS

Day-Planner Notebook

The top-of-the-line to-do list is a day-planner notebook. Sold under various names, and either paper or computerized, they have significant value to businesspeople who want to take back control of their own time. These sophisticated to-do lists require personal discipline and a sincere commitment. But they are proven tools that work.

Fine-Tune Your To-Do Today List

During the next day's 20-Minute Disappearing Act, rewrite your laundry list from the previous day in the polished form, complete with categories, delegation, and due dates. Now it's the morning and you're setting your priorities for the day. By setting the list up in your work categories, you're making sure that what's on your To-Do Today list is essential to your job. Zip those "others" off the list whenever you can! Remember, the goal of the To-Do Today list is to manage your time most effectively, not to cram in as many activities as possible. You're accomplishing two things at once when you polish your list: setting up your schedule for the day, and keeping your work load focused on doing the job you've been hired to do.

Carry Your To-Do Today List with You

Most people in business aren't tied to their chairs. In fact, some of us don't sit in a chair at all! Our jobs often keep us on our feet, constantly moving. Make sure your To-Do Today list accompanies you at all times. You want to be able to refer to your schedule at a moment's notice.

Let's say an employee has a problem and wants to see you as soon as possible; or a customer with a serious complaint calls for an appointment to see you to settle the problem once and for all; or the local high school calls to reschedule your appearance at its job fair. You need clear planning and swift action to handle each of these. You also need your To-Do Today list. A response of, "I'll have to get back to you because I'm not in my office," is a waste of time and a demonstration of indecisiveness. Instead, whip out that list, offer a time to the employee, the customer, or the high school, and move on with your day.

Update Your List with a Different Color

It is helpful to pen your To-Do Today list in one color and make all adjustments to it in a different color. This practice allows you to see the amount of replanning that happens in your day. At a glance, you will know if your original plans are continually revised. Ideally, you want to reduce the amount of revision and see less of the second color used on your To-Do Today list. The goal is to set the plan and then work on it!

> " Nothing is particularly hard if you divide it into small jobs."
>
> – Henry Ford, industrialist

Mark Off Completed Tasks

How about a little reward for all the effort you have expended developing your to-do list techniques? After completing an assignment on your list, use a big highlighter and cross it off. What a gratifying feeling! And it is so gratifying, you tend to be motivated to want to feel that way again, so back to the list you go, in search of more goal accomplishment.

You may find you have to handle tasks during the day that were never on your To-Do Today list. That's understandable and unavoidable. Maybe your boss called for a special inventory to be taken, or an unscheduled delivery arrived that had to be handled immediately. There are times that your schedule must accommodate items that were not originally on your list. We've found some people add those completed tasks to their To-Do Today lists, just to have the gratification of immediately crossing them off! How ironic—a time manager taking time to enter an already completed task. But is it such a bad practice? Probably not. The pleasure most of us get by crossing out a completed task feels so good, it can be worth the time it takes to do it. The few seconds of wasted time is a small price to pay for the sense of accomplishment we feel by physically obliterating a To-Do Today list task.

Score Your Productivity Daily

At the end of the day, spend a moment reflecting on your productivity. Look at your To-Do Today list and note how many items were completed, how many were revised, how many were moved to tomorrow's list.

Try to give yourself a score for your day's productivity. Don't over-analyze this one—just come up with a quick ballpark number as you scan the list before you prepare tomorrow's laundry list. Use a scale of 1 to 100 to measure your productivity. Mark it on that To-Do Today list.

You will be able to benchmark your productivity when you first start using this technique, and watch your growth over time. Periodically chart your scores and perform a trend analysis. By doing this very rough measure, you'll self-evaluate a very important business skill.

Periodically Review Old To-Do Today Lists

It may seem like a time waster, but archiving your old To-Do Today lists is actually a great way to become a more effective time manager. Every six months, review your old To-Do Today lists. If you've thrown them out in the past, stop that practice immediately. If yours are on paper, keep them in a binder or your planner for at least six months. An electronic version automatically retains the lists without any extra effort. Your To-Do Today lists are your record of past performance. These lists are extremely valuable in planning for your annual performance evaluation with your boss. They also act as a reliable diary that captures who did what, and when.

As you review these old To-Do Today lists, look for repeat offenders or glitches that may have skewed your performance. Is there a correlation between certain days of the week and days when your To-Do Today list changed or wasn't completed? Your lowest (or highest) productivity scores? You might be able to analyze certain activities that continuously yield underperforming days. In most cases, more information is better than less when you are trying to solve a problem. If you are not achieving the productivity level you desire, the problem can often be found in a pattern that emerges when you review old To-Do Today lists.

At the very least, you will enjoy reading what you once considered an important task. As you grow in your job, critical problems are solved to the point that they become little problems. You delegate little problems to others who are developing their skills. A review of old To-Do Today lists helps you see your own progress on the job.

SMART Goals

All entries listed on a to-do list are goals to accomplish. We advocate thinking of all your goals in SMART form:

◆ Specific

◆ Measurable

◆ Action-Oriented

◆ Reasonable

◆ Timed

All goals have a greater likelihood of being achieved if they are specifically, rather than generally, stated; measurable, as opposed to vague or qualitative; action-oriented, not philosophical; reasonably stated, not pie-in-the-sky dreams; and bracketed by time constraints, not allowed to meander indefinitely.

Here's an example from everyday life. A common New Year's resolution is to lose weight. Although succinctly stated, this goal is *not*

◆ *Specific*—it doesn't state where the desired weight reduction should occur

◆ *Measurable*—how much weight is to be shed?

◆ *Action-Oriented*—how do you plan to go about losing the weight?

◆ *Reasonable*—well, it's may be reasonable, but without knowing more particulars, it's hard to tell

◆ *Timed*—there is no time frame on how long you will take to lose the weight

Without these SMART features, the goal written as "lose weight" has little or no chance to be realized. A SMART way to rephrase the goal would be: "Lose ten pounds within six months by walking three miles a day, three days a week and eating 200 less calories a day." Breaking the goal into smaller, more manageable pieces would then allow the steps to be included on a daily to-do list. A SMART To-Do Today list task would be: "Walk three miles with the dog after work from 5:45 p.m. to 6:30 p.m." Being SMART about your goal setting is a more effective and dependable approach to accomplishing your goals.

TIME TOOLS

Cell Phone Calendar

Here's an idea from someone who is never without his mobile phone: Using the calendar function on the phone, he sets an alarm to go off at the time when he knows he'll be near the item he needs to remember. When he hears the alarm, he immediately remembers the task from his to-do list because he's right there. He handles the item right away, and it's one more task crossed off his list! And by the way, he (and many others like him) doesn't wear a watch anymore. The digital clock readout on the face of his cell phone is the new wristwatch for this modern guy.

Return of the Planner

Luckily, Logan hasn't lost her beloved friend forever. Two days after she lost the book, a kind person called her to report that he found the planner—scratched and dirty, but intact. It was next to the curb a couple of blocks away from the parking lot. Thanks to the business card tucked inside the front cover, he found her phone number. Logan picked up the planner from him and made her next stop the electronics store to buy a new PDA.

Logan has made some adjustments to her To-Do Today list routine. Gone are the paper-clipped notes, and in their place are entries on her Google Calendar program that syncs with her new PDA. Each entry is a specific task that she decides on each evening just before leaving work. She's been tackling bigger projects, now that she is able to break down her projects into smaller, distinct units. She always has the PDA with her at work, since it's so compact, and so far, she hasn't left it on the roof of her car!

Summary of Chapter Five:

One of the simplest, most basic tools of time management is the To-Do Today list. But whether or not you are a veteran list-maker, you may not be using your list effectively. Take a few minutes at the end of each day and the start of the next to review and prioritize your work for the day. This will set your focus and help you become more productive on the job than ever before.

How to Make the To-Do Today List:

1. Start with a laundry list of specific tasks that you jot down at the end of each day.

2. Use your 20-Minute Disappearing Act to polish the list, adding categories, due dates, and when possible, delegating the task.

3. Ditch as many "others" on your To-Do Today list as you can. You'll find they represent a good chunk of the extra five hours you're looking for.

4. Keep your list with you all day and revise it as work demands require.

5. Review your To-Do Today lists from time to time and use them as a check on your own personal productivity.

TIMELESS ADVICE

When you schedule your next doctor or dentist appointment, request the first appointment of the day, or if necessary, the first appointment after lunch. This way, your doctor's overbooked schedule will never ruin your day—because you're first. Remember, your To-Do Today list is important and must be protected. Let the doctor work around your schedule. After all, you're paying the bill.

CHAPTER 6

Don't Wait to Delegate

"No person will make a great business who wants to do it all himself or get all the credit."
– Andrew Carnegie, industrialist

Alex loves to talk about how he can do every job there is to do in his restaurant. Whether it's scrubbing pots at 11:00 p.m., taking apart the dishwasher to find a jammed fork, or ordering just the right amount of fresh romaine…he can do it all—and he does. Alex thinks it's important to know how to do what he asks his staff to do, as a gesture of goodwill and camaraderie. After all, how can he expect them to perform their tasks if he hasn't shown them exactly how he does them?

So he often takes over for them. If a server has a large table, he loves picking up a couple of the plates and bringing them out. And there's nothing more fun to Alex than tying on an apron, picking up a skillet, and sautéing the veggies in an order. Unfortunately, Alex finds himself taking home all of his accounting and working on the restaurant's numbers at home until the wee hours of the morning. Ordering supplies also happens long after the restaurant closes, because Alex has run out of time to do it during his regular workday. "I need more than a 24-hour day," he thinks. "There just isn't enough time to get everything done."

Delegation—The Ultimate in Multitasking

When the demands for your time seem relentless, the best tool for the job seems like multitasking. What better way is there to make the most of limited time than to do two or three activities simultaneously? If you are really accomplishing two or more tasks at once, you clearly are not wasting time.

We advocated multitasking in Chapter Four, as a strategy to better handle the distraction of telephone calls. Use a portable phone, wear a headset, or use a speakerphone so you can talk and walk at the same time. You can handle something minor while concentrating on the phone call—say, watering the plants or signing letters.

> **" Delegating means letting others become experts and hence the best."**
>
> *– Timothy Firnstahl, American business executive*

But we don't advocate trying to do more than one task that requires real concentration at the same time. That's when multitasking can be counterproductive.

Multitasking is one thing—trying to do it all yourself, all at the same time, like our friend Alex. *Delegation* is something else indeed, and it is the mark of a true time manager. The ability to coordinate several projects at once, not to do all the work involved, is multitasking through delegation. By delegating your tasks, you are leveraging yourself. "Leverage" is a financial term that refers to the power of making more money with less. You borrow money to make an investment that you expect will earn more income, thereby increasing your total. When you leverage your power through delegation, you borrow the talents of others to get more work done.

The Amish saying is, "Many hands make work light." You probably aren't raising a barn, but the same concept is applicable to your business. Use the power of others to accomplish more than you can handle on your own, and you'll get so much more out of your time spent at work.

Why Don't We Delegate More?

Many of us have difficulty delegating tasks to someone else, especially to a subordinate. We think that asking someone else to do one of our jobs, no matter how big or small that job may be, is tantamount to admitting laziness, incompetence, or defeat. All kinds of reasons have been given by businesspeople to explain why they refuse to give up tasks:

◆ If I delegate too many tasks to others, the company might decide that it no longer needs me.

◆ They pay me to do my job, not to find someone else to do it.

◆ If I want it done right the first time, I really have to do it myself.

◆ I don't want to lose control.

This kind of rationalization is the mark of someone who is insecure in his or her job. These people will never learn to manage their own time well if they don't have the confidence it takes to delegate.

Delegation Is a Manager's Function

At the other end of the job confidence spectrum are businesspeople who believe in the importance of sharing job knowledge and responsibility through the process of delegation. Not only does delegation ease time management pressures, it also builds the skills of staff members—both cost-saving activities for your company.

Effective delegation helps to develop the skills and abilities of people in your organization. In order for an employee to grow and be prepared for future promotions, the job must be a progressive learning experience. New and challenging assignments must be given regularly to prevent stagnation and foster personal development.

> " Surround yourself with the best people you can find, delegate authority, and don't interfere as long as the policy you've decided on is being carried out."
>
> – *Ronald Reagan, U.S. President*

Managers and supervisors need to offer this progressive learning experience to their staff members. They should hand out tasks that provide both a change of routine and a challenge.

Delegation Ratio

If you are burdened by 10 to 20 more hours of work each week than you want to have, adopt a one to two delegation ratio. For every extra job you are assigned, try to delegate two routine, mundane assignments you've been saddled with. The more everyday tasks you can delegate to others, the more important projects you can delve into with the extra time. You may find you don't have to be working at home or staying late every night. When you get the hours you work back under control, a one to one delegation ratio will keep you there.

Delegation Increases Your Skills, Too

When you delegate work effectively, you also increase your own job prospects. One of the key factors your boss considers when evaluating whether or not you can be promoted is who can take your place. If you have played it close to the vest with respect to delegating tasks to others, chances are your boss will decide that nobody can easily replace you. In essence, you may have made yourself too indispensable at your current job to be moved up the management ladder. But if you have developed others by delegating and assigning them projects, chances are your people have grown and are able to be promoted to fill your place as you take one higher up.

Insecure managers who don't delegate limit organizational development. These managers inevitably get passed over, while the true leaders, those who develop others through delegation, get rewarded and promoted.

IT'S TRUE

1. Time on the job is a company asset.

2. Wasting time on the job is misappropriating a company asset.

3. Misappropriating a company asset breaks company policies.

4. Breaking company policies is a terminable offense.

5. When you commit a terminable offense—you're fired.

Take the Delegation Test

Here is a simple test to determine whether you should delegate a particular task or not. If someone else who is working at a lower rate of pay than you can perform the same task with 90 percent or more acceptability, delegate it! In fact, if you don't, you are theoretically stealing from your company. Sound extreme? Hardly. Why should the company pay you $X per hour to perform a task someone else earning less than $X can do?

Start Your Delegation Engines

Here's how to get started delegating. Go back to your To-Do Today list and find tasks that someone else can do. Take the task from your list and delegate it to someone who is paid less but qualified to do it. There's a gold mine of delegating opportunities on most To-Do Today lists just waiting to be discovered.

If you can't see the opportunities right away, we'll offer some good tips to guide you. Look for some of these kinds of tasks on your to-do list, and decide who in your organization can handle the work:

Review trade journals

Often, trade journals are simply skimmed and tossed, or worse, un-opened. Many good ideas in trade periodicals are filed in the trash basket without a chance of being discovered. We feel guilty about the premature dumping of this potentially valuable resource but it can be hard to justify the time it takes to do something that seems like a tangent to our real work.

But look at reading trade journals in a new light. If the purpose is to identify new ideas, it suddenly becomes a key task, not a fringe assignment. Delegate this task to someone qualified to do it. An associate who will benefit from an opportunity to learn about your industry and ask questions about current issues is the perfect recipient of this job. Ask an associate to write a short summary of the ideas he or she discovered in reviewing trade journals each month. Now, you're developing the associate's writing skills, helping him or her learn more about your business, and saving time for yourself as well. You'll glean plenty of information from the report if you have chosen the right person to handle the assignment, and you can cross that item off your To-Do Today list permanently.

Check the competition

Evaluating the competition on a regular basis is not only a good business practice, but an essential management function as well. Whether your competitors have bricks-and-mortar stores to be investigated physically, or it requires an Internet review to see what others are doing, it's important to know what your competition is up to. But this is another task that can feel less important compared to the long list of items that shout for your attention. Some managers who can't manage their own time well enough to check the competition just rationalize, "We don't worry about what they're doing. We just focus on what we have to do." It is critical to understand our competition's strategies and how well they execute them.

> " Once a year, I write down all the regular duties I perform. Then I go through the list and ask myself, 'Can I assign this task to someone else?' I always find that I'm quite surprised at some of the simpler, yet time-consuming tasks that I can easily pass on."
>
> – Blaine Van Snick, VP,
> M5 Marketing Communications

A dedicated associate demonstrating management potential could easily be trained to do an occasional competitive check. Just as reviewing trade journals can reveal new ideas, so, too, can checking the competition. Consider it a key task to become a stimulating educational experience for someone on your staff. A short written or oral report gives you the information you need and frees up your time for other pursuits.

Plan and/or conduct meetings

Although you probably need to attend most department meetings, you don't necessarily have to plan them or even conduct them. Try training staff members in the art of conducting an effective meeting. Choose people whose jobs relate to the topic being discussed at the meeting. This will help them develop an essential management skill as well as help you by freeing up a chunk of your time.

Written communication with customers

Returning mail can be very time consuming. But take a lesson from our elected officials, whose staff members write letters and return phone calls from constituents. If your work requires written or telephone communication with customers, you can delegate those tasks to a staff member or two. Most letters can be handled with a small number of form responses, and your staff can learn how to discuss issues with customers politely. Again, these tasks can be crossed off your To-Do Today list, added to a staff member's list, and give you back some needed time.

> " The first rule of management is delegation. Don't try and do everything yourself because you can't."
>
> – *Anthea Turner, British author and media personality*

Check your To-Do Today list every day for items that others can handle. Work that is drudgery to you, or not as important as other critical tasks, may be just the assignment to delegate to staff members to help them develop their business skills. You'll gain time for yourself and make a valuable contribution to the development of your staff members.

Delegation is Not Abdication

According to the Oxford English Dictionary, delegation is "the act of entrusting authority to another person." Abdication, on the other hand, is "the act of renouncing, disowning, or casting off a job or task."

Some business people confuse the two terms. They delegate inappropriately, and end up throwing off the task without making sure it will be done properly. They abdicate rather than delegate. To delegate effectively you must know exactly what outcome you want to have, and give sufficient instructions so the person carrying out the task can achieve your aim. If your instructions are vague or incomplete, it's likely your standards will not be met.

Know the people to whom you delegate your work. If you try to delegate a job to someone who is not adequately trained to carry it out, you'll end up with a poor outcome and the task back in your lap. Don't ask an associate with limited social skills to respond to customer phone calls, for example, unless you have first enrolled him or her in a training course for speaking to the public.

Personal Delegation Grid Summary

If you have multiple staff members to whom long-term work has been assigned, you may want to keep track of the work on a Personal Delegation Grid Summary. Check your To-Do Today list for projects that others can handle and assign them accordingly. Such a worksheet can help you think through which people are best for specific assignments and to monitor their progress. Remember, you are ultimately responsible for the completion of all these tasks, so it is important that you keep track of who's doing what and how it's going. You aren't abdicating your responsibility for the tasks, just delegating the work to other qualified staff members.

Week Ending_____		
Name: _____ Task: _____ _____ _____ Due Date: _____	Name: _____ Task: _____ _____ _____ Due Date: _____	Name: _____ Task: _____ _____ _____ Due Date: _____
Name: _____ Task: _____ _____ _____ Due Date: _____	Name: _____ Task: _____ _____ _____ Due Date: _____	Name: _____ Task: _____ _____ _____ Due Date: _____

Personal Delegation Grid

The Associate Assignment Sheet

We recommend trying a simple tool to help you delegate tasks to your staff members: the Associate Assignment Sheet. This tool should be used on a daily basis. It is, in essence, an employee To-Do Today list.

Complete an Associate Assignment Sheet for each staff member to whom you are delegating one or more tasks. Hand it directly to that person and offer a brief explanation of each task. Allow the employee to ask questions about the task, to ensure that he or she fully understands what needs to be accomplished. This need only take a few minutes, and it will greatly reduce the amount of wasted time if the task wasn't understood correctly.

The Associate Assignment Sheet is a great way to delegate work to staff members who work on different shifts. If you can't explain the items personally because the shift worker is not there when you are, make sure to explain them to another supervisor who will be able to speak directly to the person receiving the Associate Assignment Sheet.

Department _____ Date _____

Assigned to	Description of Work	E.T.C. in mins	Done
_____	_____	_____	☐
_____	_____	_____	☐
_____	_____	_____	☐
_____	_____	_____	☐
_____	_____	_____	☐
_____	_____	_____	☐
_____	_____	_____	☐
_____	_____	_____	☐

Department Manager Signature _____

Reviewed by Store Manager _____ Date _____

Associate Assignment Sheet

The items you list on an Associate Assignment Sheet must *not* include fixed activities. Those kind of everyday tasks are not the same as these special items you are delegating. Everyday tasks can be permanently printed on the back of the Assignment Sheet for easy reference but should not be rewritten each day. Employees know the basics of the work that needs to be done. These Assignment Sheets are meant for tasks out of the ordinary. Knowing that the Associate Assignment Sheets are only used for variable activities keeps them interesting, and employees will appreciate that you haven't reiterated the obvious.

Entering an estimated time to complete the task gives the associate a clear indication of how far to go with a particular assignment. For example, "Clean area around the back entry" might be a variable activity entered on an Associate Assignment Sheet. Without an estimated time to complete entered next to it, a conscientious associate might spend

> " Work expands so as to fill the time available for its completion."
>
> *– Cyril Northcote Parkinson, British naval historian*

several hours doing a bang-up job outside while some of the everyday activities are ignored. If a simple, 20-minute spruce-up job is all that you want, then enter 20 minutes in the "E.T.C." column.

If a specific amount of time is not allocated to a task, associates will resort to their own judgment. But this may not be the way you expect the job to be done. Noting approximately how much time you think the job will take helps the employee understand the nature of the task assigned.

Be careful to list enough—but not too many—assignments. Allow your staff members to be able to complete the entire Assignment Sheet three or four times each week. A good rule of thumb is to assign no more than thirty minutes of extra tasks per employee per four-hour shift. That way, they will have time to do their standard duties and the few extras.

Remember the concept of SOARing from Chapter 3? You want your employees to feel that way, too. When your staff members have crossed off the items on their Assignment Sheets, they will feel the sense of accomplishment reaction. Your staff may actually look forward to their Assignment Sheets.

The overzealous manager who issues Assignment Sheets that are too onerous to complete in the time allotted will create frustration among employees and could discourage future completion of the sheets. Employees who never get to finish their entire lists may eventually give up trying.

The old story about the donkey chasing the carrot at the end of the stick is a blatantly flawed motivational theory. Eventually, the donkey has to die of starvation, never tasting the fruit of the chase! Don't fall into this trap. Allow associates to "eat the entire carrot" three or four times each week. They will be fulfilled by successfully completing all the tasks and be challenged by those one or two days when some tasks were not able to be finished. The feeling of success will be their incentive to keep trying.

You will want to make sure your employees are completing their lists. This can be handled in various ways, depending upon your workplace. You may post the sheets on a clipboard in the prep area or back room for associates' easy access, if that works for your type of business. Or you may ask your employees to check in with you once or twice a week for a quick progress report.

A huge problem retailers face is creating a motivating work environment that effectively stimulates their associates to perform. We constantly hear the complaint that associates are bored by their jobs. Hundreds of employee focus group experiences have convinced me that employees *do* want to know what to do when they don't know what to do. A carefully prepared Associate Assignment Sheet will help them know what to do, and free up your time as well.

With the Associate Assignment Sheet and regular feedback on the tasks completed, associates will become more interested in their jobs and more motivated to perform. As they accomplish their tasks with greater enthusiasm and thoroughness, fewer mistakes are made. As a result, management spends less time doing direct supervision, disciplining, and terminating of associates. The time liberated from minimizing these nonproductive activities can be used in any way you see fit!

> One cannot manage too many affairs: like pumpkins in the water, one pops up while you try to hold down the other."
>
> – Chinese Proverb

Alex—"The Delegator"

Alex finally got the message when his girlfriend started to complain about his lack of time for her. "You're always working late or taking work home to do," she said. "Why can't you get more done while you're at work?" He realized that taking on so many jobs himself left him unable to do what he needed to do. His employees weren't growing in their jobs, either. So he vowed to make some changes.

A month later, Alex is on his way to earning a new nickname: "The Delegator."

The pile of trade magazines he'd been tripping over for six months are now being read by an assistant manager who told Alex she wants a career in food service. Alex gets a short report from her with ideas from the trade journals every two weeks. His customer letters are being answered by a young cashier who is working his way through college. He is both computer-savvy and a competent writer. Alex looks over a sampling of the letters written each week to be sure the tone is correct.

Alex has stopped jumping in to take over in the kitchen. Instead, he cross-trains line cooks to help the sous chef so they will learn more food preparation techniques. The clean-up crew especially enjoys the Associate Assignment Sheets. The special tasks break the monotony of their work and make them feel they are contributing to the whole operation in a meaningful way.

His newfound authority and ability to delegate jobs to others has given him the confidence to examine his own schedule more carefully. He now weighs jobs and decides if they need his attention. When he delegates an assignment, he reviews the job when it is completed.

Alex is starting to feel that he is finally gaining some control over his professional life.

Alex had an amazing experience shortly after starting to delegate work with Assignment Sheets. One late afternoon, he tried to leave work a little early to participate in a Wednesday evening golf league. As he opened the door of his car, he heard his name. A hostess in the restaurant and one of the back-office staff approached Alex and asked about their Associate Assignment Sheets.

Apologetically, Alex said he hadn't completed the sheets for their shift because he was leaving early. They seemed disappointed and said they would fill out their own sheets, and walked back into the restaurant. Alex could not believe what had just happened. Did two employees just go out of their way to ask for more work?

They weren't the greatest employees at the restaurant, Alex realized. Rather, they were average workers who had displayed only average initiative before he implemented the Associate Assignment Sheets. Now, because of the direction the sheets provide and because of the constructive interaction employees have with him each time their sheets are reviewed, they actually look forward to being assigned additional work!

Summary of Chapter Six:

Even when you know how to do everything at work, you can't do it all. Delegating jobs to others accomplishes two very important goals: freeing your time and developing your staff. You shouldn't fear that others will learn what you know; rather, you become even more valuable when you are able to supervise more work by delegating to qualified people.

How to Delegate:

1. Check your To-Do Today list for work that others can handle. Sometimes tasks that you would like to do but never seem to have time for are perfect to delegate to staff members.

2. Delegate tasks with a formal Associate Assignment Sheet.

3. Be sure that the person you delegate to can handle the job. Consider delegation to be a good way to develop staff members' job skills.

4. Don't overwhelm people with more tasks than they can accom-

plish in the time frame you need the job done. Employees will enjoy handling special tasks if they are successful at completing them.

5. Delegate all jobs that don't need to be handled by you. If the task can be done by someone who earns less than you do, then you aren't the right person to do that job. Put your time and efforts toward work that needs your personal attention.

TIMELESS ADVICE

Think "Peel 'N Stick." Peel off tasks you can delegate from your To-Do Today list and stick them on other lower-paid, qualified assignees. It's a win-win!

CHAPTER 7

Never Accept
the Baton

*"Time is the coin of your life.
It is the only coin you have,
and only you can determine how it will be spent.
Be careful lest you let other people spend it for you."*
– Carl Sandburg, American author and poet

*L*ogan was really excited about going to the sold-out Dave Matthews concert Friday night. She had bought the ticket months ago and was planning a fun evening with friends. But that afternoon, one of the employees in her department came into Logan's office with some bad news. "That spreadsheet you asked me to work on isn't finished yet," she said. "I had some trouble finding all the information. Here's what I've gotten done so far. I know you needed it by today, so I'm giving you as much as I could do."

Logan was furious, but didn't have time to argue. The spreadsheet was part of a larger project that Logan's boss was working on, so she had no choice. She called her friend and reluctantly told her to give away the ticket. She now had to work late that night to complete the spreadsheet.

"Why does this always happen to me?" Logan thought. "I try to delegate work to other people, but it always comes back to me incomplete or incorrect. And then I'm the one responsible."

Unfortunately, Logan now has the task back on her To-Do Today list. She needs to hold her employees accountable for the work they are assigned.

> *Otherwise, the jobs she delegates seem to be in a revolving door, which keeps spinning right back around to Logan. Not only is this task taking more of her time at work, she's losing out on her weekend time, too.*

Staying in the Race

In Chapter Six, you learned how delegating tasks gives you more time by using your resources wisely. By handing off jobs to others, you save that time for jobs you need to handle yourself. At the same time, you're helping your employees develop new skills. Sounds like a win-win for everyone.

But not if your employees bring the tasks back to you.

Think about delegating tasks as a relay race. As the runners complete each leg of the race, they pass the baton to the next runner on their team. At the end of the race, the last runner holds the baton, triumphant.

You'll notice that baton never goes backward. The runner of leg #2 doesn't get to pass the baton to the runner of leg #1. The baton only goes forward, until the race is finished.

As a manager, your job is like the coach of a relay team. During the race, the coach is on the sidelines, watching, shouting instructions, and encouraging the team. But the coach never accepts the baton from the runners. In business, the manager gives an assignment to the employee who has to complete it (run the distance) or pass to another person (hand off the baton to the next team member). The employee should never return the assignment to the manager until his or her leg of the race is complete.

Playing Piggyback Is for Kids

Did you enjoy playing piggyback as a child? Carrying a friend around the yard was fun. But as a manager, you don't want to be carrying your employees. Your goal is for your employees to complete the tasks assigned to them without needing you to finish the work. Almost nothing slows a manager down more than accepting an incomplete assignment or condoning partial performance. *You* have to finish the work or find someone else who can.

There's another children's game that's appropriate here. It's called, "I'm rubber, you're glue. Whatever you say bounces off me and sticks to you!" If you are a manager who is successful at delegating tasks, you may have been good at this game and uncomfortable with piggyback rides. Whatever you assign should stick to the person to whom the task has been delegated until the assignment is complete, and never bounce back to you.

Employees will quickly learn that if they make a simple attempt to complete the task, they'll be able to give it back before completion when the going gets rough. They will lose the important sense of personal responsibility.

When employees experience fewer successes because they don't see projects through to closure, you limit their development of a sense of self-worth. You also lose the opportunity to foster learning. When employees

> " President Wilson...was, by all odds, the hardest worked man at the Conference; but the failure to delegate more of his work was not due to any inherent distrust he had of men—and certainly not any desire to 'run the whole show' himself—but simply to his lack of facility in knowing how to delegate work on a large scale."
>
> – Joseph Patrick Tumulty,
> Woodrow Wilson As I Know Him, 1921

are presented with new challenges, they are learning experiences that further development. By letting them off the hook, they learn less.

TIME TOOLS

The 30-Minute Portable Project

Carry at least 30 minutes of work with you at all times. There is always a delay, a line, or an unscheduled stop at some point in your day. If you plan for those productivity holes and fill them with a low priority task you carry along, you'll use your unscheduled free time wisely.

Reading trade journals is a great way to fill productivity holes. They are an essential part of many jobs, but most people don't take the time to read those magazines. Knock off trade journals while waiting in the car to pick up your kids from soccer practice or on a half-hour metro trip.

Whenever you use those unscheduled productivity holes, you're finding more of those extra five hours a week!

How to Handle the Baton Pass

What is the best way to handle an employee who tries to pass a task back to you? How do you keep from taking the job back on to your To-Do Today list, just to make sure it gets completed? Like poor Logan, you may be responsible for handing a whole package to your boss, and that unfinished piece of business will reflect badly on you if it's not completed.

Resist the urge to solve the problem for your employee. If you become the problem solver, you take back the baton and undermine all the progress you've made with that employee. Sure, you may be able to do the job yourself—you probably can, quicker and more thoroughly than the person you delegated the task to—but you'll have one more item to add to your list and your employee will miss out on the learning experience.

Require your employees to present at least one possible solution to any problem that they bring to you. If you make this a blanket policy in your office, you'll find more and more people developing solutions to problems that are effective and creative.

Ask people to recommend at least one solution when they have reached an impasse. It may not be a workable solution in the end, but they will begin thinking as problem solvers.

Ask one of these questions when an employee comes to you with an unfinished project or a problem: "What do *you* think is the best way to deal with this issue?" or "What would *you* do to solve the problem?"

If you require your employees to come up with a possible solution, you can discuss the employee's idea right away. In most cases, the employee's idea will be a reasonable one. Praise the idea and get them working on a solution to the problem.

When people brainstorm, one of the primary rules is there can be no negative comments during the brainstorming part of the meeting. Ideas are allowed to flow freely and without judgment. Critiques come later, when all possible ideas have been developed. At the start, the mission is to help everyone think of possible solutions.

This same kind of mechanism is at work when you require people to come up with a solution to any problem they may bring to you. It doesn't have to be the best one, but you want your employees to start thinking in terms of *solutions* rather than *problems*. When an employee knows that he or she needs to bring a solution to you when there is an issue, the juices toward solving the problem start flowing. You can discuss the task at hand in a positive way, using the employee's solution as a springboard. You can help the employee develop his or her idea further, and set the employee back on the task to finishing the project.

You won't be tempted to take the problem back, because the employee has already started to consider possible solutions. You are there to help your employee find the best solution and complete the work without your interference. Like a coach, you give encouragement and guidance, but you don't score the goals or run the race.

Give your people the chance to prove themselves, develop new skills, and solve problems. In the process, you'll free up some of your own time, as well.

"Hedgehogs" and "Weasel Words"

I have a name for employees who try to pass the baton to other people without completing the job: "hedgehogs." They hedge on their commitments, trying to back out of tasks assigned to them. They are closely related to another difficult animal in the workplace, the "weasel." Weasels and hedgehogs don't work hard at their tasks—they work hard at getting out of doing them! You'll recognize hedgehogs and weasels by the things they say. Listen carefully and work diligently to change their behavior for the sake of the organization and your To-Do Today list.

Hedgehogs and weasels must learn new ways of talking on the job.

They'll often say:	But they need to say:
I think I can	I know I will
I'll try to	I will do it by...
I hope to be done by...	It will be completed by...
Maybe	Certainly
It's likely I'll...	I'm sure I'll...
I ought to have it by...	I'll have it no later than...
By the end of the week	Friday, 5:30 p.m.
Probably	Without a doubt
If all goes well I should...	You can count on it by...
Sometime tomorrow	10:20 a.m. tomorrow

We can't run a business on terms of vagueness. Hedgehogs and weasels can derail, confuse, and delay any project. An alert manager can preempt their tactics by stepping up and challenging these common phrases and their lack of commitment. When confronted by employees who are evasive or noncommittal, ask them to rephrase their statements using one of the firmer phrases that won't allow them a loophole. In the long run, these employees will develop greater pride and a sense of accomplishment in their work and you may find some of your extra five hours.

Be There for Guidance

There are times when an employee needs a manager's expertise to finish a task, but too often managers are eager to grab the baton and run with a project before their involvement is warranted. Your job as a manager is to encourage your employees to pursue the task they undertook to its conclusion. Let them know that you are looking forward to their final presentation. Mention that if they have any difficulties along the way, they should ask for guidance. Add that you are counting on them

IT'S TRUE !

"I was promoted and took over management of a large store with 130 employees. I worked my tail off for eight months to prove I could handle the job. Working 75 hours or more each week, I was the go-to guy. People called me on the intercom, came up to me instead of others, called me at home. I felt needed and important.

But I woke up one day and said 'I can't do this anymore.' I was simply worn out. I started delegating profusely to my two assistants and stopped being the person who handled everything. I started answering questions with questions. I began focusing more on leadership qualities and development of a team. The store sales began growing by double digits.

The moral of the story? I was holding my team back by being the go-to guy, and burning myself up in the process. By allowing my team to make more decisions on their own, they learned much more, while I gained back the time I needed to run the store without the store running me."

– *Tom Schulte, Vice President of Operations, B&R Stores, Inc.*

to complete the assignment. Give your employees all the tools they need to complete the task, but don't do it for them. Everyone will benefit and the whole team's performance will be stronger.

Creating Checkpoints

Our friend Logan assigned a task to an employee, and at the end of the week, it was dropped back in Logan's lap incomplete. Logan was surprised to find that the work had not been done, and she paid the price by forfeiting her own leisure time to finish it. She needs to help this employee stay on track and teach the employee responsibility for assigned work.

TIME TOOLS

Sample Form Letters

Maintain sample letters of the kinds of issues you need to use on a regular basis. These previously used letters have worked well at solving their intended purpose. No need to continuously create new ones. Use them over again. You can change the pertinent information quickly, print the letter, and the process takes just a few minutes.

One way to make sure your employees won't bring the baton back to you is to establish a system of checkpoints along the way to help them monitor their progress on the task. If you assign a task with a due date of one week out, don't wait for the final day to find out how the work is going. Set up a checkpoint midway through the week. A short meeting with you and the employee will address these issues: (1) review how much of the job has been completed so far, (2) find out if there are any unresolved questions about the problem, and (3) suggest additional resources that may be needed to complete the task. Ten minutes is probably sufficient.

If a project is more complex with a longer time frame, several checkpoints will be useful to be sure things are going smoothly. It's like a ship captain checking the radar every so often to make sure the boat is still on the charted course. If it has veered off track a bit, it's easy to redirect. But if the captain waits too long, the ship may run aground.

> " Have milestones and checkpoints for all projects you have a project plan for. It goes to ownership and accountability."
>
> *– Ken Pink, President, E.W. James & Sons*

Managing Your Boss

Now you know what to do when someone who you have given an assignment to tries to give it back to you. You simply work with your employee and make sure the problem doesn't happen again. But what about the situation when your boss asks you to take on a task that you can't fit into your schedule? How do you keep from accepting that baton?

Start by asking a few questions. What is the due date? What is the priority of this task? How does it fit with the rest of my workload? Explain that if you drop everything to handle this project, you'll have to postpone tasks A, B, and C. Is that acceptable? Your supervisor will be impressed that you have such a firm command over your To-Do Today list and will help you prioritize the new task or assign it to someone else.

Even more difficult is the situation of a superior, but not your direct superior, assigning a task to you. Think before you agree to accept the assignment. Even if the work is something you'd enjoy doing, you must first assess your regular workload and assignments given to you by your direct boss. Your first responsibility is to that person, who will likely be miffed that you put off his or her work in favor of someone else's assignment.

Here's how to handle the situation: "Thanks for thinking of me to handle this assignment. I have a pretty full plate at the moment, so I'll have to check with my boss first to confirm that I can postpone something she has given me so I can get yours done according to your time frame. I'll get back to you by four o'clock, after I have spoken with my boss." This tells people you are willing and able to take on the job, but that your responsibility to your direct boss is your first consideration before you add to your To-Do Today list.

When you're ending a meeting with your boss, make sure someone goes over the *Who?* is going to do *What?* by *When?* questions before you adjourn. If your boss doesn't do it, you should ask those questions so everyone at the meeting knows task responsibilities.

Sometimes It's Okay to Say No

Get comfortable saying no when someone tries to pass the baton to you. Of course you want to help, get the job done, be a team member. But you can't—and shouldn't—take on all the problems in the office.

When someone comes to you with a task that is unfinished and wants you to take it on, stop and think about your own schedule first. What's already on your To-Do Today list that needs to be completed? If you take on this additional task, can you do an effective job with the rest of your work? Will other tasks you currently are responsible for suffer when you add this new one?

Often it's not one of your own staff members who brings an incomplete job back to you. One of your peers at work will try to talk you into accepting a job that you don't want or have time to do. That's when you really need to learn how to say no.

There are plenty of pleasant ways to turn someone down. "I can't help you this time because I'm busy with ____." "I have another commitment at the same time, so I won't be able to participate in ____." "I'm completely booked for the next two weeks and can't take on anything new until after that time." "Have you asked ____?" (Suggest someone who is qualified and may have more time available.)

If you have set your priorities on the tasks already on your To-Do Today list, it will be easy to say no when someone tries to add another task. You don't want to do a mediocre job, but that's what will happen if you try to take on too much.

No More Batons!

When the weekend was over, the work completed, and the concert missed, Logan decided it was time to make a change—in her own behavior. She vowed to help her staff get the job done without taking it over herself. She will never again accept an incomplete assignment from one of her employees.

Her first order of business was to institute a money jar for all weasel words attempted during her department meetings. Anyone trying to hedge or weasel was fined two dollars per infraction. Logan used the money to help fund their year-end holiday luncheon.

Next, she gathered her staff together and let everyone know what she expected of them. "I want to encourage a positive attitude in this department," she began. "From now on, when someone has a problem and needs help, I want you to think of at least one possible solution to the problem before you bring it to me or anyone in the department. We're going to become a group of problem solvers."

Logan gave her staff an example of how the new policy works. "I had the assignment of developing a new rate schedule," she explained. "When I hit a wall with some of the research, I wanted to go directly to my boss and tell her that I had done as much as I could do. But first, I thought about talking to people who had done this before. I suggested that idea to my boss, and she directed me to a couple of people who have had experience with a similar project. They helped me find what I was looking for, and I was able to complete the rate schedule." Logan became a problem solver and she is now on the way to building a whole department full of solution-minded folks.

"I need time to work on my To-Do Today list projects," thought Logan. "Finally, I'll stop taking on everyone else's to-do's, too!"

Summary of Chapter Seven:

Delegating work is a key component in your plan to manage time more effectively. But what do you do when employees don't follow through on their assignments? If you agree to take the project back and finish the job, you are adding to your time burden, not helping to relieve it.

A smart time manager gives employees the tools they need to complete assigned jobs. That way, when they need help, they don't return with the task unfinished. Creating a culture of problem solving rather than problem passing ensures that everyone follows through on the job.

How to Keep from Accepting the Baton:

1. Delegate jobs wisely. Try to be sure the person who receives the assignment is well equipped to handle it.

2. Bring a solution to the problem. Require that if someone brings a problem to you, he or she must also come up with at least one possible solution to the problem first. This way, you're immediately discussing solutions, not problems.

3. Remember that your job is like that of the coach—you provide guidance, encouragement, knowledge, and experience. But like the coach, you don't run the race for your team.

4. Practice what you preach. Make sure you provide solutions to problems that you need to take to your boss, as well. Employees will see you modeling the behavior you want them to adopt.

5. Don't be afraid to say no. Assess your own priorities first before you agree to handle a new responsibility.

TIMELESS ADVICE

Eradicate the "weasels" and "hedgehogs" from your workplace. Do it professionally, methodically, and expeditiously. They may serve a purpose in the wild, but they are not good in a purpose-driven work environment.

CHAPTER 8

Make Meetings Meaningful

*"Meetings are indispensable
when you don't want to do anything."*
– John Kenneth Galbraith, economist

*A*s a new manager, Logan is responsible for a group of thirty employees who report directly to her. She loves to talk one-on-one with each of them, but repeating the same information thirty times just isn't an efficient use of time. So Logan calls meetings whenever she has something she thinks is important to discuss. Everyone just drops what they are doing and troops into the break room when Logan emails them that a meeting will take place in a half-hour.

As she walked by the break area the other day, Logan overheard several of the employees discussing the recent meetings. "Another meeting? What a waste of time!" said one employee. "And what's the point, anyway?" asked another. "We talk and talk, and nothing ever seems to get done." The third employee said, "I'm not showing up to the next one—I have too much work to do and I don't want to have to work late to catch up from the time we waste in the meetings."

Logan shrank away from the break area, embarrassed by the comments. She thought it was helpful to hold meetings so she could let the employees know about important news. "Maybe I need to rethink how to bring everyone together so our meetings are worth the time it takes to hold them."

Meetings and Time Management—Oxymoron?

Why does the topic of holding a meeting belong in a book on time management? Because meetings take a lot of our time at work, and we don't want our time to be wasted.

There are endless jokes about meetings as time-wasters:

◆ Lonely? Want to meet people on company time? HOLD A MEETING!

◆ Sales are off 12 percent at XYZ Company. But meetings are up seven percent!

Meetings should be more than a necessary (or unnecessary) evil—they should be a valuable way to communicate.

When meetings aren't handled properly, they are far more than aggravating. The company loses productivity and wages during a wasted meeting, multiplied by all the people who are in attendance. If the meeting has five people, add up all the wages of the five attendees to see what the meeting really cost the company. If there are 20 people at the useless meeting, add up 20 wages…well, you get the idea. To say nothing of the opportunity cost of being at the meeting rather than doing something else more productive. Meetings should be an investment of time for everyone participating, with the return being the value of the communication.

Even worse, each successive bad meeting leads to diminished value of future meetings. When employees remember that past meetings were a waste of time, they anticipate the same for the next meeting. You may find fewer and fewer employees choosing to participate in meetings as a result.

But the tarnished reputation of meetings is regrettable. The power of a well-executed meeting can be incredibly stimulating. Here's what can take place in 60 to 90 minutes during a well-run meeting:

◆ Thoughts can be shared

◆ Ideas can be developed

- Problems can be identified and solved

- Rumors can be squelched

- People can be informed

- Assignments can be delegated

- Mutual respect and understanding can grow

- Opinions can be changed

- Information can be quickly disseminated

- Praise can be given

All this from a meeting? Yes, indeed—in a professionally conducted meeting.

What is going wrong at so many meetings? Why isn't every meeting we attend valuable and worth the time it takes?

The most common mistake people make when holding a meeting is poor or no pre-planning. Holding a meeting without a predetermined outline or agenda is like playing football without a game plan. It can be done, but chaos and loss are the most likely outcomes.

When a meeting isn't planned ahead of time, it can easily turn into a free-for-all. If topics are not

> " You now have my whole philosophy of business, born at ABC, nurtured at Paramount, and perfected at Disney. It is this: Call meetings about subjects that really matter—and show up!"
>
> – *Michael Eisner, founder, The Tornante Company, and former Chairman and CEO, The Walt Disney Company*

specified ahead of time, anything is up for discussion. You can't say, "That item isn't part of today's agenda" if you haven't established and distributed an agenda before the meeting. It can be very hard to limit discussion of a topic when a time frame hasn't been set. Employees will resent being cut off if you tell them, "We have to stop discussion on this topic now," if you haven't specified how much time will be spent on each topic in the meeting.

Even managers who remember to set the topics for the meeting often forget to prioritize those topics. If you are organizing the meeting, you know what you want to get done, and those priorities should be reflected in your pre-planning.

One of the worst mistakes people make at a meeting happens after the meeting. Managers often fail to follow up on the issues that were agreed on during the meeting. This happens when the manager doesn't summarize at the end of the meeting what are the next steps. Without establishing the Action Plan, how does anyone one know *Who?* will do *What?* by *When?*

Failing to follow up on what went on during the meeting demonstrates to all the attendees that the time spent together was wasted. People spoke, people listened, but when it was over, nothing was done. It's not hard to figure out why no one would want to participate in the next meeting.

TEAM Meetings

As a manager, one of your most important jobs is to keep your employees working as a team. Communication is a key to maintaining a team, and structured TEAM meetings are a great way to facilitate that communication on a regular basis. TEAM stands for "Thoughts Exchanged by Associates and Management." Institute regular TEAM meetings to keep the communication flowing.

These meetings should help you save time, not waste it. But if you want to incorporate meetings into your time management arsenal, you need to handle them properly. Meeting management falls into four areas:

1. General Preparation
2. Set Up for the Meeting
3. At the Meeting
4. After the Meeting

Let's look at each area and detail what is important to do for the best time management of your meetings.

1. General Preparation:

Choose a location.

Choose a distraction-free meeting place. If your employees can hear the sounds of others working during the meeting, they will be less likely to give the meeting their full attention.

Commit to regularly scheduled meetings.

For many businesses, we recommend monthly meetings to keep communication flowing in the workplace. Set a specific regular meeting date and time for the entire year. The fact that regular meetings are scheduled and time is being carved out for them shows employees how important these meetings are to the organization. Let employees know exactly what day and time your meetings will be held every month by posting a twelve-month calendar in the employee break room or other appropriate spot. This will allow employees to plan ahead.

Choose meeting times and dates.

Choose the best time for your workplace to hold meetings. For retail businesses that are busy on weekends, one of the best times to schedule meetings is Thursday at 4:00 p.m. Usually, most employees are at work that day. Fridays involve heavy pre-weekend activities, and Saturday is out of the question. Monday, Tuesday, and Wednesday usually have fewer employees scheduled to work. By Thursday, the operation has a full contingent of employees at work, so you have a greater chance of higher participation rates.

For companies with traditional shift workers, 4:00 p.m. may be a good meeting time. Day shift workers can leave their jobs an hour early, attend the meeting, and go home. The night shift can come in an hour early, attend the meeting, and report to work. In your workplace, it may be better to rotate the time of your scheduled meetings to give all employees an opportunity to attend as many meetings as possible each year.

2. Set Up for the Meeting:

Prepare a plan.

You should spend about as much time preparing for your meeting as it will take to hold it. A 20-minute meeting means you should plan it for 20 minutes. Longer meetings require more planning to make sure the meeting is well worth everyone's time. What are the objectives? What issues will appear on the agenda? In what order should they be presented?

Provide an outline.

Give attendees an outline of the meeting's objectives a day or two before the meeting. Everyone wants to know what to expect in a meeting, and attendees will be able to prepare their thoughts or gather background information with advance notice. They may even be able to contribute to the agenda.

Limit attendance.

Try to have five to fifteen people in attendance at most meetings. Fewer than five employees limits input and synergies. Meetings with more than fifteen tend to become unwieldy. A good rule of thumb: if you can't read the facial expressions of every participant, you probably have too many people in attendance. The seating arrangement is also important. Try not to use an auditorium or classroom-type of seating

> **I always plan the outline of a meeting and stick to it!"**
>
> – *John Dietrich, Store Manager, Ossege IGA*

setup. Shy people and newcomers tend to slip into the background and get lost in the crowd. A circular, rectangular, or horseshoe-shaped seating arrangement works well to keep all the participants in the loop, physically and psychologically. Attendees will feel as though they are part of the meeting and participation will increase.

Limit length.

Most meetings should last no more than ninety minutes. The agenda should be limited to eight issues. Each issue should take no more than ten minutes of meeting time. If you adhere to these limits, your meetings will keep moving and finish on time.

Remember, shorter is usually better when it comes to meetings. Sometimes a fifteen-minute meeting that addresses only one or two issues is far more effective than a long meeting with many items on the agenda. A regularly scheduled, brief meeting where a single issue is discussed may be useful to keep your group on track.

3. At the Meeting:

Greet attendees.

Greet all meeting attendees as they arrive. Make your greeting cordial, but brief. Ten minutes of storytelling will only add wasted time to the meeting. A businesslike start immediately sets the tone that the meeting is important and worth everyone's valuable time.

Give a printed agenda.

Distribute a printed copy of the final agenda to everyone as they enter or have it displayed on a flip chart. The formal agenda sends an important message—this is an organized, results-oriented meeting. It also helps to keep the meeting on track. Latecomers will be better able to get involved without having to disrupt the proceedings.

Start and end on time.

Demonstrate your commitment to careful time management by starting the meeting promptly—when it is scheduled to start—and ending the meeting on time. When you dawdle before beginning the meeting, or allow the meeting to drag on past the time set on the agenda, you signal that time isn't important. End on time even if you haven't been able to complete all your agenda items. You can make those unfinished items the first ones on the agenda for the next meeting.

Review the ground rules.

Before beginning a meeting, always go over the ground rules. We're not talking about Robert's Rules of Order here—you can save those for your board meetings. Ground rules control the proceedings and let everyone

IT'S TRUE

Lauren Dixon, of Dixon Schwabl Advertising in Rochester, New York, has found a novel way to discourage unwelcome comments when trying to get meeting participants to brainstorm ideas. Everyone at the company's staff meetings comes armed with a water gun, which they are instructed to squirt at anyone who has negative comments. According to Dixon, "It helps them be more comfortable because no one will be criticized or scrutinized."

– Emily Maltby, "Boring Meetings? Get Out the Water Guns," the Wall Street Journal, *January 7, 2010* know how the meeting will be conducted. You determine what your ground rules are for your meetings, then review them at the start of every meeting. You don't need many; just decide on a few that you think are important to help keep the meeting running smoothly.

Two ground rules that work in most meetings: One, limit the amount of time each participant can speak on any given subject to two minutes or less. This way, you'll avoid a filibusterer who rants on and on, enjoying his or her own voice but not adding to the discussion. Two, ask participants to reserve personal issues for a one-on-one discussion at another time. This will help keep the discussion businesslike and avoid topics that are inappropriate for the whole group. We don't want to hear about Sue's problem with her paycheck during a meeting.

Record the proceedings.

Choose someone to write down the important points of the meeting. To give everyone a chance at the job, you can use the selection of the recorder to act as a meeting icebreaker. Spin a bottle, like the old game. When the bottle comes to rest, it is pointed at the note-taker. This engages everyone instantly. You may prefer to choose someone to act as the recorder before the meeting, and let that person know ahead of time.

Regardless of the method you use to select a recorder, it makes sense to rotate the person, so someone different has the responsibility at each meeting. Often, the recorders don't have the opportunity to contribute their own ideas to the meeting when they are busy taking notes.

There are several ways the notes can be taken. A large pad on an easel

TIME TOOLS

Speakerphone

Invite key people in on the conversation and you won't lose time having to repeat it.

can be an effective way to keep track of the major topics discussed during the meeting. The recorder notes the key items of discussion, and everyone at the meeting can see what has been said. As sheets of paper are filled up, they are ripped off and taped to the walls. This works especially well in a brainstorming-type meeting, or one where ideas are coming fast and furiously. Some recorders may prefer to take notes on a laptop computer. This can be very useful to summarize the meeting and send it via email to everyone shortly after the meeting is completed. Still others may use the tried-and-true technique of keeping notes by hand on a notepad. Any of these methods work well, as long as the recorder pays attention and captures the most important items from the meeting.

Maximize participation.

When it's important that many people have a chance to weigh in on the discussion, begin with a volunteer and proceed around the room clockwise or counterclockwise to include everyone in order. No one can be left out using this procedure. Those who do not wish to comment at a particular time can simply pass. The two-minute maximum ground rule ensures that no one monopolizes the discussion. A tip to increase participation is for the group leader to ask that everyone first write down his or her response to a particular question or idea before anyone speaks. That way, the more reserved individuals in the group can read their responses rather than having to speak extemporaneously. Maximizing participation while minimizing embarrassment is key here.

Maximize attention.

It's smart to begin the meeting with old business from the previous meeting. Then move to the issue that involves the most people in the room. Bump the topics that involve the smallest number of participants to the bottom of the list. This ensures maximum interest and attention. Make it your practice to ask a random participant to stay for five additional minutes at the end of each meeting to help you evaluate the meeting's effectiveness and to review his/her notes. Knowing this is your standard operating procedure, all participants will become infinitely more attentive and more thorough note-takers.

Delegate during the meeting.

Your employees will often offer excellent ideas during a meeting. But that doesn't mean that you have to load your To-Do Today list with new projects. Instead, solicit the help of others in the meeting to take a rough idea and flesh out the details. During the meeting, ask for volunteers to work on the idea or assign an associate or two to the project. People will be energized and excited about the new idea, and they will be ready to work on it right away. Make sure the recorder notes the idea and names of the people who will be working on it so they receive the recognition. Adding a time frame for the work to be completed holds them accountable, as well.

Summarize results.

The final few minutes should be reserved for summarizing the meeting's accomplishments in relationship to its stated objectives from the agenda. Spin the bottle again to select a person to give a summary of the meeting. If your people are aware of this practice, they will stay engaged throughout the meeting and take careful notes because they'll know there's a chance they'll be called on to give the meeting's summary. Ask that the summary be given in the form of *Who?* is going to do *What?* by *When?* All participants will leave the meeting with a clearer understanding of the next steps.

4. After the Meeting:

Communicate results.

Communicate the results of your meeting to everyone who needs to know, both meeting attendees and employees who did not attend. Use whatever communication technique works best in your workplace— email, memo, or hard copy posted on the employee bulletin board. Make a commitment that the notes will be available within 48 hours.

Follow up.

Make sure you follow up on the ideas and projects delegated during the meeting. If you have set dates for completion of those projects while in the meeting, this will be easy to do: simply enter the due dates on your calendar to monitor results. Another way to handle follow-up is to have the people assigned to the project report on its progress at the next scheduled meeting. Make that report one of the first items of business at the next meeting.

If you have taken responsibility for an item brought up during the meeting, make sure to communicate the results to everyone interested. Nothing turns people off meetings faster than if an item discussed at a meeting suddenly disappears. If it was your responsibility to follow up, don't forget it. Your employees are sure to remember.

If you post the notes from the meeting in a visible place, such as the employee break room, you can easily post the follow-up results. As items are completed, cross them off the list. If more information is needed, post it right next to the meeting notes. Brief email messages are another great way to let employees know that you have followed through on an item from a meeting. You can also give a quick update at the start of the

> " My laptop computer has added significantly to my productivity. I use the laptop at meetings for the recorder to take notes. Since the agenda is already created, it is the outline, and the recorder types comments beneath each agenda item as it is discussed. Meeting notes can be distributed to all concerned parties shortly after the meeting. Notes are more complete and they can be easily read!"
>
> *– Kyle Westover, Sr., Director of HR, Kiddie Kandids*

next scheduled meeting to inform the group of the progress made on last month's items.

When you let your employees know what has been done regarding suggestions and agenda items from one meeting to the next, you reinforce the purpose of having meetings. It reminds your staff that meetings don't have to be time-wasters. If handled properly, meetings can be part of successful time management.

Alternatives to Meetings

You only want to have a meeting when there is no better way to communicate with your group. If you can email the information, or provide it in any other way, do that. A meeting is to share information, not just to disseminate it. One-way communication is *not* a meeting—it's a seminar, a lecture, or a rant.

TIME TOOLS

Meeting Cost Calculator

Think how much each meeting costs in terms of the salary of each person in attendance. A meeting that lasts a few hours and has 20 participants can cost the company more money than you might expect, if you added it all up. A new device called Bring TIM does just that—it calculates the salary cost of every person attending a meeting and totals it to illustrate exactly how much each meeting costs. Invented by a manager who found himself in four-hour staff meetings, the device makes it obvious that "time is money."

But actual meetings, where everyone gets together in the same room, are not always the best use of time. If the people who need to meet together aren't physically located together, it will cost a lot of time and money to transport them all to be in the same room at the same time. Consider virtual meetings via video or audio conferencing. A variety of technology exists to make virtual meetings easy to accomplish.

IT'S TRUE

In an effort to communicate information, I scheduled a bi-weekly meeting on Friday afternoons with the sales staff. The purpose of the meetings was to meet and communicate about current and prospective customers. In a short period of time we would all know what is going on throughout the company. The goal was to meet each time for one hour. The first few meetings failed miserably. The first took over three hours due to my lack of preparation. I ended the next meeting at one hour, but we never communicated anything. Then I tried to have a written agenda with handouts at the meeting. We went two and one-half hours.

We have finally found a good mix. We changed the meeting to Monday afternoons, and I distribute the agenda on Friday afternoon. We now get through the meeting in 45 minutes.

– *Bill Bradshaw, VP of Sales, Buxton*

For two or three people, video conferencing can take place while all the participants sit in front of their computers. Applications such as Skype and iChat provide free conferencing services for two or three participants. Even a three-way conference telephone call can substitute for a face-to-face meeting, cutting time and expense. Instant messaging services such as Yahoo! Messenger and Windows Live Messenger allow people to "chat" by typing messages to each other that are more quickly sent and received than email messages. Smart phones can access these services, so people can interact with each other from almost any location.

For larger groups, video conferencing equipment and software is available. While some companies choose to own this equipment, others make use of video conferencing centers that have the capability of receiving and transmitting video to everyone signed in to the system. Companies with multiple offices can hold virtual meetings that allow any number of associates to participate simultaneously.

Regardless of the technology used to orchestrate a meeting, the same rules apply. A meeting doesn't have to be a waste of time. It can be a serious competitive weapon and time maximizer when properly administered.

Meetings Back on Track

When Logan was invited to attend a meeting conducted by another department head, she saw first-hand how productive and motivational a meeting could be. A clear agenda was given, with specific time frames for discussing each item. Projects were delegated to meeting attendees, and Logan even volunteered to handle one. At the end of the meeting, the department head summarized what had transpired during the meeting and continued to inform them in the days that followed as the agenda items were completed.

Logan immediately sat down and created a meeting calendar for the next year, taking into account her employees' schedules. She developed a clear agenda for the first scheduled meeting and distributed it two days before the meeting date in order to get feedback as well as topic suggestions.

At the meeting, she set time frames and goals, and concluded the meeting when she had promised. Two employees were appointed to work on a couple of issues that arose during the meeting. Logan is following up with them to make sure they have completed the assignment in time for a report at next month's meeting.

"I used to hate going to meetings," Logan thinks. "Now that I'm the one holding the meetings, I have to be sure everyone who attends doesn't think they are a waste of time, as I once did. If I plan and run the meetings right, I'll also have more time in my day."

Summary of Chapter Eight:

Gathering the troops for meetings is usually the best way to keep communication open in the workplace. But too many meetings waste time because they are unplanned, unstructured, and unproductive. When you use meetings wisely, they can be tremendous time maximizers that let you disseminate lots of information and receive feedback efficiently.

How to Hold Meetings:

1. Plan meetings ahead of time. Set times, dates, and agenda items so everyone involved can be prepared.

2. Take charge of your meetings. Limit how much time to devote to each agenda item, and hold attendees to the schedule.

3. Delegate items that need more work to attendees during the meeting. Have a recorder keep track of who is responsible for what and when the results are due.

5. Let everyone in the department know what happened during the meeting, including those who were unable to attend.

6. Follow up on the items covered during the meeting and inform people when items brought up during the meeting have been completed or resolved.

7. Make sure a meeting is the best way to communicate. An email message or memo is usually better for one-way messages. Save meetings for times when sharing of information and discussion is key.

TIMELESS ADVICE

For impromptu meetings, paper and pens should be offered and available for all participants. For scheduled meetings however, it's interesting and revealing to see who attends your meeting without bringing paper and pen. What would possess someone to come to such an exchange without note-taking tools? What are they saying (silently) about the value of your meetings?

CHAPTER 9

Careful Recruiting Saves Time

*"You're only as good
as the people you hire."*

–Ray Kroc, founder, McDonald's Corporation

*A*lex doesn't like it, but he finds himself spending a major part of each day covering for irresponsible no-shows or working with employees who just can't seem to do their jobs correctly.

"Today I spent twenty minutes going over for the third time how to use the computerized order system with one of the waiters," says Alex. "He keeps making the same mistake that messes up the cooks in the kitchen, even though he had plenty of training on the system."

"Then I had to intervene when a customer was unhappy with the way she was treated by one of the hostesses," he continues. "She seemed personable when I interviewed her, and we were really short-staffed when she was hired. Now I'm starting to think she has no interpersonal skills at all!"

"But most of my day today was taken up with a huge legal hassle," he says. "I hired a delivery guy who was recommended by a friend of a friend. His DUI charge while using a company car to deliver an order is costing us a fortune—my time, our legal counsel, not to mention the bad publicity we've received in the local paper."

Alex has a big problem that goes far beyond the infringement on his time. He doesn't have an effective way to hire great employees, so his staff includes too many poor performers. Between his time spent on hiring replacement employees and his coaching and reprimanding of employees who just don't "get it," Alex contends he spends close to 90 percent of his day on people problems. "Why can't I find employees who are able to do their jobs without my constant supervision?" thinks Alex.

The Reason for Careful Hiring

Time management for business people must take into account all of the tasks a manager must do on the job. We've tackled the obvious time-wasters: lack of planning, workplace distractions, poor organizational habits, trying to do it all yourself, and pointless meetings. But if you want to reclaim at least five wasted hours each week, examine the amount of time you spend dealing with avoidable issues with your employees.

- ◆ "How many times do we have to go over the procedure for entering new clients into our database?"

- ◆ "I've had another report about your unprofessional behavior from other employees."

- ◆ "This company prides itself on superior customer service, but I just saw you ignore a customer who clearly needed help."

Every time you have to deal with an employee over some kind of personnel issue, you are taking time away from other work. Cutting down the number of issues you have to work on with your employees would help you find more time in every day.

What's the best way to lessen the amount of time you have to spend on these kinds of tasks? Take the time that's needed to hire the right people for the jobs to begin with.

Most managers agree that over 75 percent of their time is directly or indirectly spent dealing with the results of a bad hire. Making the wrong hiring decisions means there will be problems, large and small, that will occupy much of one's time at work. A front-end employee who doesn't smile at customers; an accountant who refuses to learn the latest software and insists his tried-and-true methods work best; a construction worker who distracts the rest of the work crew with jokes and stories all day. If you are the supervisor or manager of any of these employees, you will spend considerable time talking, cajoling, disciplining, retraining, and hoping. Your time could undoubtedly be spent doing more productive tasks.

> " People are definitely a company's greatest asset. It doesn't make any difference whether the product is cars or cosmetics. A company is only as good as the people it keeps."
>
> *– Mary Kay Ash, founder, Mary Kay Cosmetics*

Turnover Counts

When a business has high employee turnover, an additional time-waster is the number of interviews and exit interviews that must be given to keep replacing employees. Is your amount of turnover necessary? There must be a better way to recruit employees to ensure that less time will be spent in the future dealing with personnel problems.

Very few companies measure their turnover and review trends in the data. Even fewer use this data as input in a manager's performance review. But the amount of employee turnover can be very telling about both the manager's skills and the way employees are hired for the job. Management usually assumes that turnover is inevitable. While a certain amount of turnover is unavoidable, it is important to understand where the cutoff point is between normal turnover and too much turnover. Start by making an effort to determine how much employee turnover is appropriate and how much is too much.

Recruiting Nightmares

Most companies devote remarkably little effort toward developing a competent recruiting process. It's often an unstructured process, with forms that collect little information about the applicant.

Recruiting well requires making a sincere effort to place the proverbial round peg in the round hole and the triangular peg in the triangular hole. When are we going to learn that putting an introvert in a position with heavy customer contact, or a vegetarian in the supermarket's meat department, or a creative type in an assembly-line job are all exercises in futility? You want to utilize your employees' talents. Doing so requires that we find people whose abilities really match the job description.

When an employee doesn't work out, we waste even more time on the exit interview and the process to find a new employee to handle the job. Most terminations are the result of management's inability to fit the candidate with the demands of the job.

We all hope that the people issues in business will eventually clear themselves up or go away. But there is nothing that hangs on longer than a problem employee who has made it into the company and proceeds to poison it with a poor attitude. One bad apple rarely spoils the whole bunch, but it definitely ruins those near it. That type of employee rarely does anything bad enough to warrant termination. Usually, you just live with the situation unless something major happens.

Job Profiling

One of the best ways to improve your odds of finding the right employee for a particular position is to profile the job you are trying to fill as thoroughly as possible. Every aspect of the position should be defined clearly. For example, the profile should answers questions such as:

- ◆ Is the job full- or part-time?
- ◆ What specific skills does an applicant need to perform the job?
- ◆ How much prior experience in the field is needed to do the job well?

Every job position in your organization needs a clear job description, which is important for determining pay scales and dividing the work to be done among various positions. But a job description can also help the person who is hiring find the right individual to fill the position. How can you hope to hire someone who will perform well in the job if you aren't knowledgable aboutwhat the job entails?

The job description also tells the applicant what will be expected if hired. When applicants know the specifics of each position, they can evaluate which jobs are best for them.

Applications 101

Make sure the application is designed to answer the questions you need to know. A "one size fits all" application may be easy, but it could also be too general to unearth the most important information for some jobs.

Have ample applications available at your workplace. Don't tell applicants, "I can't find any applications now. Can you come back?" That's a sure way to turn off potential employees and send them to the business down the road. Provide a comfortable location for the applicant to complete the application. Potential employees should be given the opportunity to put their best foot forward, which includes being able to complete the application thoughtfully, either at your location or at home.

Let the applicant know when he or she can expect to hear from you. Give the applicant a timetable for when a decision will be made, and then stick to it. Remember, this is someone's job—someone's livelihood— and they deserve the respect.

Everyone in your organization should know how to handle an application properly so it isn't lost or misplaced. This often happens in smaller companies without a personnel department assigned to handle initial employment applications. Institute a procedure for everyone to follow so applications get to the right person right away.

Source List

The most effective recruiting process begins by identifying your most productive labor pools. Knowing where the pools are located saves time and frustration. Determine where you are likely to find the most qualified applicants and continue to tap into the most lucrative sources.

TIME TOOLS

Rolodex

Whether on your computer or the traditional card file, a Rolodex gives you quick, alphabetical access to hundreds of resources and frequently used contacts.

Every business will have its own sources, but some are universal. Your source list for qualified applicants is likely to include:

- Current employees
- Customers
- Educational institutions (depending on the jobs, these could be high schools, colleges, graduate schools, or technical training programs)

◆ Relatives, especially in a family business

◆ Window signs

◆ State employment services

◆ Competitors

◆ Classified advertising

◆ Vendors

◆ Social clubs (e.g., seniors, 4-H)

◆ Trade associations and magazines

◆ Government-funded agencies

◆ Military agencies and veterans outreach

Analyze Your Sources of Applicants

List all the possible sources that generate applicants (e.g., window sign, newspaper ad, etc.) in a small space on the back or bottom of your job application. List the sources with a check box next to each. Ask the applicant to check the source that motivated him or her to apply.

Once a year, analyze the information to see which sources generated the most interest. Then review the application forms from the best applicants and note the sources of those people. You may find that just a few sources generated 80 percent of the applicants and one source in particular generated five of the best applicants you hired all year. With this knowledge, you will be able to focus your recruiting efforts on the most productive labor pools, which will enable you to spend less time and money in the overall recruiting process.

The Mini-Application

For companies who hire many entry-level employees, the mini-application is a useful recruiting tool. Edit your application down to the most essential questions and ask applicants to complete that mini-application first. You'll save time—yours and theirs—by screening out candidates who are obviously unsuitable. For example, if your workplace requires weekend hours and a candidate indicates he or she is unavailable Saturday and Sunday, you can immediately reject the applicant without wasting more time on a more extensive application or interview. You'll need much more information to know if you want to hire an applicant, but a few basic questions can help you pare down the pool of applicants quickly.

Think of this process as a way to market the jobs at your workplace to potential employees. Like most of society today, applicants are time-starved. Why insist on a lengthy, time-consuming job application before it may be necessary? Applicants will appreciate this quick pre-screening method, and if they make the cut, then they can complete the full-length application.

> I make the decision whether or not to hire someone during the job interview. I count the number of times they smile. If it's enough, they're hired."
>
> – Senator Feargal Quinn, founder of Superquinn and former President of Eurocommerce

Interviewing

Another way to expedite the application process is to try a mini-interview. After the applicant completes the mini-application, ask him or her for three more minutes to meet a manager or supervisor.

Some applicants will be apprehensive about this suggestion, because

JOIN US!

We hope you've noticed the fine individuals who work here. We take pride in selecting the best people available. If you are interested in joining our team, complete this quick application.

NAME _____ DATE _____

ADDRESS _____

CITY _____ ZIP _____

PHONE: DAY _____ EVENING _____

POSITION DESIRED _____

2nd CHOICE _____

HOURS AVAILABLE

	FROM	TO
MONDAY		
TUESDAY		
WEDNESDAY		
THURSDAY		
FRIDAY		
SATURDAY		
SUNDAY		

Thank You for Your Interest in Us!

Mini-Application

they probably had not anticipated meeting a manager. Allay their fears and encourage the candidate to take the time to do so.

The mini-interview should take place in a quiet area, but not in a private office. An office interview is apt to snowball into a 15-minute inquisition. The mini-interview can even take place with both parties standing. After a brief introduction to break the ice and establish eye contact, ask the following three questions:

Question 1: "Why did you come in today to apply for a job with us?"

The key word is "us." You want to establish the level of interest and sincerity in working with your particular team. Would any job suffice or do they really want to work with you?

After asking the question, the manager carefully listens and watches the applicant, looking for facial gestures and listening for inflection in the voice that may offer clues to the applicant's true motives for applying. On hearing the response, an attempt should be made to score it, on a scale of one to ten. Ten is an awesome, sincere, and enthusiastic response. One is a negative, apathetic, or sarcastic response. Keep the score in your head for now. Later you can mark the scores on the application if the applicant is asked to return for a second, more thorough interview.

What's a number ten answer to the question of why the applicant is looking for a job at your company? "I shop here all the time and it looks like everyone working here is having such a great time. I am looking for part-time work, and I feel I'd really fit in."

A number five response? "I need a job with flexible hours and I happened to be walking by and saw your sign."

An answer that merits a zero? "I need a job, and this looks like easy work. Besides, my mother told me to get out of the house."

Question 2: Ask the applicant why your company does something specific that he or she would be familiar with. For an entry-level supermarket job, for example, the question, "Why do we verbally offer customers a choice between paper or plastic bags before checkout?"

would be appropriate.

The response to this type of question requires some thought. It gives some insight into whether the applicant understands something basic about the job. In the supermarket example, will the applicant be customer-minded and respond, "So the customers are satisfied when they leave the store?" That's a ten-point answer. Or, will the applicant respond, "Because that's what the handbook says?" Five points. Or worse, "So the customers don't complain afterwards." That's a zero-point response.

Then go to Question 3: "Did you notice...?" Fill in the blank with something in the workplace that the applicant probably won't know, but would know soon after starting work. This presses the applicant to lie, to tell the truth, or to improvise. Observe his or her facial reaction.

> " Doing a job badly and then getting someone in to sort it out can be much more expensive than getting someone in to do the job properly in the first place."
>
> —Sarah Beeny, real estate developer

Will the applicant be so intent on making a good impression that he or she guesses in an effort to provide an answer? That's not what you hope to see—zero points. Or is the applicant honest enough to respond, "I don't know, but I could find out. Just out of curiosity, why did you ask me that question?" That's a 10-point answer to an off-base question, and shows the applicant can probably think on his or her feet.

A mini-interview gets company management involved in the recruiting process early. It is also very useful for getting a quick read on the applicant's personality. Question 1 covers sincerity; question 2 gives you information on whether the applicant has a basic feel for the business; and question 3 gets to the critical issues of honesty, curiosity, and initiative.

Total the score. Out of 30 possible points, how did the applicant fare? The insight you glean from the mini-interview may help you choose which candidates you should call back for a more comprehensive interview.

The next time you have an opening to fill and dread the process of por-

IT'S TRUE !

> Sir Richard Branson took an innovative approach to hiring in his semi-spoof 2004 television show, *The Rebel Billionaire*. It's not a realistic interview venue, but the idea makes a lot of sense.
>
> His contention: it is important to know how a job applicant reacts to an underling. Branson disguised himself as an elderly cab driver and picked up potential applicants from the London airport to take them to the interview. Along the way, he got a good look at how each applicant behaved with the cabbie. Not surprisingly, two potential contestants who were condescending to the "cab driver" (Branson) were immediately kicked off the show.
>
> Wouldn't it be fun to try that next time you're interviewing for new employees?

ing over 10 or 20 applications, remember the mini-application, mini-interview, and scoring process. These timesaving ideas will enable you to call in the most promising applicants based on their responses to just a few critical and probing questions. If we begin our recruiting process with better applicants, the quality of the employees we ultimately choose will improve.

Keep the Final Decision Within the Department

The best person to decide who gets hired is the manager closest to the job opening. In other words, if a part-timer is needed in the warehouse, the warehouse manager should make the final decision on who is chosen. Of course, personnel departments and higher management can and should act as filters to screen the applicants carefully. But the choice between the final three or four candidates should be up to the manager who is ultimately responsible for the success of the employee.

The reason for this is ownership. If the department manager makes the decision on who is chosen, he or she will take ownership and work diligently to make the employee successful. If the department manager is handed a new employee from personnel, there is a tendency to treat the new recruit as an outsider who was someone else's selection. If that employee fails to make the grade, it's easy for the department manager to blame someone else. Instead of working hard to make the selection of the new employee successful, the department manager has a built-in scapegoat, someone to blame, and less incentive to make the relationship work.

The Full Interview

The thorough interview is designed to probe into the personality of a candidate to determine whether there can be compatibility between the applicant and the job. This is the interview that should be conducted by the decision maker closest to the candidate on the organization chart.

Ask introspective and probing questions. A lot of talking doesn't always

IT'S TRUE

> Here's a unique screening method actually used by a retailer as part of his overall evaluation process. Once introduced to an applicant at the front of the store, the owner invites the prospective employee to follow him to his office back through the warehouse. Halfway through the store, the fast-paced owner stops and turns to see how far behind the applicant is following. The distance between the two is his gauge of how well the applicant will be able to "keep up" with the business!

indicate a productive conversation or interview. Open-ended questions can reveal much about the candidate in a short period of time. The following are examples of questions you might use in your full interview:

- ◆ What were your biggest work and non-work accomplishments over the past two years?

- ◆ What two things did you especially like about your previous job? Dislike?

- ◆ What goals have you set for yourself this year?

- ◆ What new skills or capabilities have you learned over the past year?

- ◆ What one thing is most likely to make you lose your temper?

- ◆ What were the biggest pressures on your last job?

- ◆ What type of criticism was given of your work by your previous employer?

- ◆ If you were in a position to make changes regarding your previous job, what two changes would you have made?

◆ What do you feel are your three strongest abilities, and how would they relate to our position?

◆ What do you like to do when you are not working?

◆ What do you need to know from us in order to determine whether or not you can handle this job?

◆ From your point of view, what three things do you consider most important to make a company a good place to work?

◆ Is there anything about your work or conduct we should know before contacting your previous employer?

◆ What makes you distinctly qualified for this position?

Select your favorite five or six questions from this list. Use the same questions in every interview. Over time, you'll find that high performers respond similarly, as do those less likely to succeed.

Track Your Success

Some managers are better at interviewing and selecting new employees than others. Why not make it a practice to determine who is better at selecting the best from the available pool?

The first step is to track who is responsible for each selection decision, then ascertain who were the top candidates chosen during a given period. Simple analysis will identify which managers are better at this crucial process than others. Once you have identified them, allow those managers to be more involved in the recruiting process.

Retention begins the moment words are exchanged between the candidate and the company. Personality assessments through informal and formal interactions begin instantly. Managers must have a clear understanding of what the job requires as well as the insightful questions to determine the needs and desires of the candidate. When they do match up, you just might find yourself with that perfect fit.

IT'S TRUE

> What do the best college sports teams do? Recruit the best players all the time! When a business is short-staffed, that is the worst time to recruit because you are desperate. It is much better to recruit and network all the time, so the pipeline is full when you need it. Just like college sports teams, when you recruit the best you get a reputation for excellence and great players (employees) want to be on your team. Recruiting gets a whole lot easier when you have a reputation for being a great place to work.
>
> – Joanna Meiseles, "Six Keys to Running a Successful Business," Great Entrepreneurial Minds blog, posted November 27, 2007

Recruiting Carefully Is Time Well Spent

Alex has learned his lesson when it comes to recruiting more carefully for all of the positions in his restaurant. He makes sure that a background check of each applicant is performed before a job offer is made. "We could have saved so much time and money if I had checked on that delivery guy's driving record," he thinks.

His front-of-the-house supervisor and the kitchen supervisor take the lead in hiring employees now, using specific techniques and questions that the management team have collectively agreed upon. They screen out candidates quickly so that they have more time to devote to full interviews that really help them identify who is best for the job. Best of all for Alex, turnover has significantly declined over the past six months, and the entire operation is running smoother. Alex is delighted when he sees such tremendous improvement, "I can't believe how much less time I'm spending on employee-related problems."

" The best executive is the one who has sense enough to pick good men to do what he wants done, and self-restraint enough to keep from meddling with them while they do it."

– Theodore Roosevelt, U.S. President

Summary of Chapter Nine:

One of the biggest drains on a supervisor's time is dealing with employees who have problems on the job. The only way to combat this effectively is to hire the right people for the jobs in the first place. A little effort on the front end will save you lots of time on the back end.

How to Recruit the Best Employees for Your Positions:

1. Profile each job. Write a thorough job description so everyone involved in hiring understands the job responsibilities. Detail the education and experience necessary for the job. Understand all the characteristics that will make someone successful at the job.

2. Pay attention to your application process. For many companies, applying for a job is an afterthought of management. Make this process work for you—not against you.

3. Know your best sources of applicants. Keep track of how your best employees find you and use those sources more heavily when looking for new applicants.

4. Use the mini-application and the mini-interview to screen out undesirable applicants quickly. You'll whittle down the group of potential employees to a manageable size with a small investment of your time.

5. Choose five or six open-ended questions to ask at every interview. You'll learn how the best employees answer them when you ask a standard set.

6. Keep the hiring process within the department as much as possible. The person who will be managing the new employee has the most at stake and will work hardest to make sure a new hire is the best fit for the position.

TIMELESS ADVICE

If your employees are truly your greatest assets, it's logical that your To-Do Today list should include some activity that raises the value of these assets, such as a TEAM Meeting or a Performance Update.

CHAPTER 10

Discipline Progressively

"Discipline is the bridge
between goals and accomplishment."
– Jim Rohn, author and speaker

*L*ike many young managers, Alex wants to be liked and accepted by the employees at his restaurant. After all, he grew up with most of the associates he is now supervising. One of his least favorite parts of the manager's job is disciplining an employee who breaks company rules.

Today Alex is wrestling with a problem. "Chris is late again," he thinks, noticing that one of the servers hasn't shown up for his morning shift. "I guess I'll have to talk to him. This is the third time he's been late." Alex made a mental note to do something about Chris, but in the meantime, he has to find someone to fill in. He checks with the house manager, who places a call to Julie, one of her long-time employees. She persuades Julie to come in, even though she doesn't usually work on Tuesdays. Right after the problem is solved, Chris comes in, about 40 minutes late.

Now Alex has another problem. He has two servers working a shift that only requires one. He and the house manager have wasted more than 30 minutes troubleshooting the problem. He has to pay Julie extra for her time. Alex is really angry with Chris. He calls Chris into the office and says, "If you're late again, I'm going to have to let you go! This is at least *the third time and I'm really losing it with you. You just don't get it, do you? You've got to play by the rules."*

Chris is shocked by Alex's rampage. "Alex, you've never said anything about being late before," he replies. "All the servers always cover for each other when we're a few minutes late in the morning. It's no big deal."

Alex doesn't know how to respond. He knows Chris has been late before and he hasn't said anything to him. He knows the servers help each other out when they need to. But he also knows that Chris's lateness today has cost Alex both time and money, and he doesn't want it to happen again. Who wasn't following the rules—Chris or Alex?

One Bad Apple...

Disciplining employees causes a great deal of wasted time for managers. The time wasted is hard to see at first, and only becomes obvious when the problem gets so big it can't be ignored. Then a manager must spend a great deal of time and effort trying to correct the problem—time and effort that could have been put elsewhere if the discipline process had been handled properly right off the bat.

One bad decision leads to another and another. One overlooked problem leads to someone else doing the same thing, and then another person, and another.

An employee who acts in an improper manner, or breaks company rules, or is a negative force in the workplace can influence co-workers to do the same and bring down the morale and performance of other employees. An effective discipline system that deals with issues as soon as they arise is the best way to take back the countless hours you may be wasting on problem employees.

What are you doing (or not doing) that may require you to spend a lot of time cleaning up the mess later? Like our friend Alex, most managers avoid confrontation with an employee who has caused a problem. Instead of dealing with the situation, they resort to any number of justifications and excuses. Managers often ignore the first time or two that an employee breaks a company policy, especially something that is not a major problem. Some people use humor or sarcasm to try to convey disapproval. Other managers indirectly punish the offender by giving the employee the worst shifts or the worst jobs, hoping he or she will just go away and thereby avoid a confrontation.

But ignoring a problem doesn't make it disappear. As we all know, it usually gets worse, and then we spend a lot of time trying to correct it. The answer is to institute and follow a disciplinary process so every employee knows what is expected and what the consequences of poor performance will be. When a simple discipline procedure is followed, it takes very little time and results in major time savings by eliminating the need for further discipline, firing procedures, or ultimately, recruitment of a new employee as a replacement.

Research on "Bad Apples"

A study of employee "bad apples" showed that in workplaces with a team member who was toxic or negative, the team members were much more likely to have conflict, have poor communication and refuse to cooperate with one another. Consequently, the teams performed poorly. They also found that negative behavior outweighs positive behavior—that is, a "bad apple" can spoil the barrel but one or two good workers can't unspoil it.

One of the authors of the study, Will Felps, recommends that companies take greater care when hiring to screen out potential "bad apples." And when someone is found to be a negative force in the workplace, he recommends that disciplinary measures be taken, up to and including dismissal when necessary.

Source: _"How, When, and Why Bad Apples Spoil the Barrel: Negative Group Members and Dysfunctional Groups," Will Felps, Terence R. Mitchell and Eliza Byington,_ Research in Organizational Behavior, _Volume 27, 2006_

IT'S TRUE

Business consultant Donald Todrin tells the story of how one "bad apple" spoiled the work environment and negatively affected the performance of the workplace.

The employee was a tow truck driver who was using company equipment to work for a second company, collecting paychecks from both and cheating his employers.

For one month, company performance was down, although no one could understand why. Workers were not dependable, they bickered, they didn't handle their paperwork properly—in general, everything at work suffered.

When the "bad apple" was finally discovered, he was fired and the workplace immediately began to improve. Within a few days, the workers were back on track and revenues increased dramatically.

Todrin says this was the strongest evidence he has ever seen that it takes just one person doing the wrong thing to affect the whole group.

– Donald Todrin, Let's Talk Business blog,
posted September 5, 2008

In fact, managers with experience are quick to point out that when employees are in an environment where disciplining is swift and fair, the problem employee generally snaps into shape (or quits) and the desirable performers produce more.

Managers are often intimidated by the person they need to discipline. Perhaps the associate occupies a valuable position in the company. The manager may think that employee would be very difficult to replace. "She might quit if I discipline her! Then what will I do?" Don't capitulate to this kind of workplace blackmail, whether overtly expressed by the employee or just implied. No one is irreplaceable, especially someone who may be negatively influencing the rest of your staff.

The ABCs of Addressing a Performance Problem

Sometimes what may seem like an issue that requires a disciplinary step is actually an issue of training or motivation. Give the situation the ABC test to determine if it is in fact a true disciplinary problem.

ABC: Awareness—**B**uy-In—**C**apable

To determine if the problem you are experiencing with an employee is performance-based, consider the following.

Awareness: Is the employee aware of the problem or deficiency? If not, it is up to you to make him or her aware of the problem.

Buy-in: Did the employee buy into the procedure, policy, or idea? At some point (at the orientation meeting, for example), did the employee understand that the job would entail the specific policy or procedure that is now causing difficulty? If not, consider a reorientation for this employee as a first step toward rectifying the situation.

Capable: Is the employee mentally and physically capable of doing the assigned task(s)? If not, consider retraining or repositioning the employee. If the associate is perfectly able to complete a set task, but chooses not to, it is most likely that the situation requires the D step—disciplinary action.

The Five-Step Discipline Process

Managers are often reluctant to discipline an employee, even when it means that others in the group may be affected by poor performance or behavior. We think that's because most managers don't really know how to discipline in a way that is easy, quick, relatively painless for everyone, and works.

The Five-Step Discipline Process has been designed to address the most common stumbling blocks to effective employee discipline. This system works in both union and nonunion organizations, and it works with employees at every level of the organization. Implementing the Five-Step Discipline Process will give you more time in your average workweek, by handling problems quickly before they mushroom into something larger that will ultimately require more attention.

We'll describe each step, using Alex's scenario with his tardy server. The process gives procedures for managers to handle disciplinary problems in a positive and efficient manner.

STEP 1—Quick Verbal Warning

Alex just learned that Chris, a server with one year of experience, came in late this morning. This is his first time arriving late to work. As soon as Alex sees Chris, he calls him over to a corner of the workplace. "Chris, may I see you over here for a moment please? I need to speak with you." That's it. Nothing more alarming than that. This step is a simple conversation in a quiet corner of the workplace, *not* Alex's office.

Step 1 is purposely designed to be easy on everyone, to ensure that it actually takes place.

Here's the kind of conversation that takes place in Step 1:

> ALEX: "Chris, I noticed that you came in late today. Did you know that you were late?"
>
> CHRIS: "Yes, I did."

ALEX: "Did you call in to let someone know you would be late?"

CHRIS: "No."

ALEX: "During orientation we discussed the importance of being on time. On page 12 in the Employee Handbook, we talk about calling in if you're going to be late. Why didn't you call?"

CHRIS: "Well, I thought I could make it..."

ALEX: "Chris, you're important to us and you are a good member of the team. Do you know why we ask you to call in if you're going to be late?" *(Note: This is an important question. Wait for the employee to answer.)*

CHRIS: "Well, it's probably because you don't know whether I am going to be in at all, or if I am just running late. You're not sure if you should call a back-up person or not."

ALEX: "That's right. In fact, I have Julie here now. She gave up her day off to come in and replace you. Now that you're here, what should I do? Send you home? Send Julie home? Luckily, I have something for both of you to do, but it's going to hurt our payroll. All you needed to do was to call us one hour before your start time. That could have avoided this whole situation. I hope you understand now, Chris."

That's all there is to Step 1. Just a three- or four-minute conversation and then, "Let's get back to work."

No formal write-up is done at Step 1. This is key, because it puts the infraction in its proper perspective—important to take notice of and correct, but not a major breach of company policy. However, make sure you write down the date when you had the Step 1 conversation, for future reference if necessary.

The failure to discipline is partly a result of a widely held notion that any discipline action must involve a write-up. This is too intimidating for many managers, and instead, they often avoid dealing with the minor infraction.

TIME TOOLS

Index Cards

These are handy notepads. Don't lose that thought. You'll be frustrated when trying to think of it later. They are small and easy to carry in a pocket. Don't be caught without something to jot a note down on when you have that brainstorm or think of an action you need to take. And, of course, a pen!

Step 1 is simple. Any manager can do it, even those who may be hesitant or insecure about disciplining. It is also the most critical step. Discipline must take place the first time it is needed. The first time an employee makes a mistake regarding any policy that is spelled out by the company, he or she must be spoken to, no matter how minor the mistake or how likable the person. The first infraction simply cannot be ignored.

If a manager ignores the first infraction, or even lets the situation continue until the associate has committed the same mistake two or three times, it is very difficult to play catch-up.

In the situation described at the start of the chapter Chris had come in late several times before Alex decided to discipline him. At that point, Alex was angry. He called Chris into his office and said, "Do you know that you have broken a company rule three times over the last few months?"

Chris thought, "What's wrong with Alex? I've only been late a couple of times. Anyway, I always stay late and I never complain. And Alex never said anything about being late before."

By not saying anything the first time Chris was late, Alex set himself up. By being reluctant to discipline, he made it seem that the issue was not particularly important. Now Chris feels that Alex is being unfair. "After all," Chris thinks, "If he really cared about it, he would have said something before."

If he were to take this matter further, Chris would probably gain the support of any arbitration panel. Alex didn't follow the rules. He didn't stand by the guidelines established in his company handbook. How was Chris to know that the issue was so important?

STEP 2—Verbal Warning in the Office

Chris is late to work again. It's been one month since the first time he was late.

At this point, Alex should say, "Chris, may I see you in my office for a few minutes, please?" Once in the office with the door shut, He should begin to discuss the lateness. "Maybe you thought I wasn't serious the last time we spoke about the importance of company policies. Do you understand the policies in the Handbook?"

The main difference between Steps 1 and 2 is that Step 2 occurs with you and the employee in your office. You are still pleasant and respectful, not condescending or out of control. Once again, there is no written disciplinary note. The conversation should progress similarly to the first one, with the employee recognizing that being on time is important to everyone at work. Once again, note the date of this Step 2 conversation.

The subtle progression from Step 1 to Step 2 helps managers and supervisors who are timid about disciplining an employee. These steps move gradually from the casual to the more formal. It's much more comfortable to have a conversation than to formally document the employee's infraction the first or second time. By following these two simple steps, a manager establishes control and authority over the situation.

STEP 3—Written Record of Office Conversation

Two months go by and Chris is late again. The third step is to speak with him again in the office, and this time to document the infraction in writing.

Alex may want to consider having another manager present. If the workplace is unionized, it may be a requirement to invite the shop steward to attend disciplinary meetings in Step 3, Step 4, and Step 5.

Again, Alex should discuss the late arrival and the fact that this is Chris's third infraction. Discuss the specific company policy that addresses lateness and the consequences the company takes when an employee is late. Chris should be given a chance to explain why he was late, but Alex should use his judgment to assess the validity of the excuse.

At this step, Alex needs to document the conversation in writing and make sure the employee knows he is doing so. Here is an example of the type of memo you can write to document Step 3:

Memo To: Chris Smith
Re: Company Policy Infraction
From: Alex Stevens
Date: January 7, 2010

On Jan. 7, 2010 I spoke with Mr. Smith about his arriving 40 minutes late to work. This is the third time he has gone against company policy. We have already discussed the issue on Nov. 2 and Dec. 10, 2009. Mr. Smith said he will not do this again and that he will try to improve. He understands the reasons for the policy and how we administer it. I stated that I was sure he could improve, and advised him that if he broke company policy again, he would probably be suspended.

Note that the dates of the previous infractions are included. They are not formally recorded until Step 3. This reinforces to the employee that Step 3 is an official notice. Steps 1 through 3 give the employee three chances before more serious steps are taken.

STEP 4—Suspension

Unfortunately, two months later, Chris is late again. He must be called back into the office. Here's the conversation that takes place this time: "Chris, I've had to write you up again. This is the fourth time we have talked about an infraction of company policy. I'd like you to go home and think about whether you are capable of and willing to adhere to our company policies. Remember, these are policies you agreed to when you joined our company. You signed off that you accepted the policies. Two months ago, when we met, we wrote up the infraction and you promised that things would change. Now, here we are again. I'm not mad, but I am very disappointed with your behavior. Please go home now and write down a two or three-paragraph action plan that will convince me your behavior is going to change this time. Be very specific, please." Then Chris is sent home for the day.

> " Discipline is a form of training. Although self-discipline is the goal, sometimes counseling or progressive discipline is necessary to encourage self-discipline."
>
> – Fred Ball, CEO, Ball Super Food Stores, Kansas

Hopefully, Chris will come back the next day with some positive ideas for improvement in his written action plan. Maybe he will suggest buying a new alarm clock, or leaving the house 40 minutes earlier every day, or asking to work the night shift. By suggesting in writing options like these, Chris is demonstrating that he really wants to keep the job. If, however, he returns with a paper that reads, "I will try harder," Alex will know that his commitment isn't very deep. If he doesn't bring in any action plan at all, that's a good indication that Alex should begin to plan for a replacement.

Suspending an employee is a very serious action to take. It is taken only after the three previous attempts to change behavior have been exhausted. The suspension demonstrates a progressive next step in the disciplining process. The intent is to alert the employee to his or her current poor performance and give the employee 24 hours to think through the entire situation, in the hope that he or she will arrive at a plan to improve performance.

The suspension action is not intended to punish. It is meant to rehabilitate or reorient an employee to the policies and procedures already explained several times before. In most suspensions, we strongly urge managers to pay a suspended employee for the scheduled shift. If not, the employee will no doubt harbor resentment for losing wages, despite the fact that it was his or her fault for getting suspended. If a manager suspends an employee for one day, during which the employee is paid to think over the positive actions needed to take to improve behavior, the results of the suspension will usually be more fruitful.

A suspension is a definitive, corrective action management must use to enforce policy and procedures. And this progressive step must occur before termination.

STEP 5—Termination

The fifth meeting with Chris is the third time for a formal written documentation of the meeting. After the fifth time Chris is late, Alex's conversation in his office should be something like the following: "I'm sorry you find it so difficult to change your behavior. I have done everything I could to get you back on track to no avail. So, effective immediately, you are no longer an employee of this company. I have an exit survey for you to fill out. Your final paycheck will be ready on Thursday. I would also like you to sign this third memo detailing the nature of your infraction."

Termination is never easy, but this process of progressive discipline is reasonable. The first steps are relatively easy to administer and by the time Step 5 comes around, a manager will feel little hesitation about taking positive action to terminate because he or she has followed the progressive procedure and tried repeatedly to help the employee change his or her behavior.

When to Use the Five-Step Discipline Process

There are three basic categories of infractions: Not Serious, Mildly Serious, and Terminable.

The Five-Step Discipline Process is designed to best deal with the "Not Serious" category, which accounts for the majority of infractions. Examples of this type of infraction might include coming in late, not wearing the appropriate uniform, or not greeting a customer properly.

If an employee is rude to a customer or has broken a piece of company equipment because of on-the-job neglect, one might be inclined to proceed directly to Step 3, passing Steps 1 and 2. Of course, terminable acts such as stealing, drug or alcohol use on the job, or abusive behavior toward a customer or fellow employee would result in a Step 5 action, forgoing Steps 1 through 4. You should use your judgment on when all five steps should be employed, but also spell out clearly in your policies those infractions that will result in immediate termination.

An infraction that is not serious is not irrelevant. In fact, most infractions that are not serious, if left unchallenged, will develop into more serious ones.

The Five-Step Discipline Process is analogous to a warning you might receive the first time you are caught driving at 40 mph in a 25 mph zone. With a little luck, you'll be stopped by a police officer who understands the value of a verbal warning. The police officer decides not to write a ticket this first time, and instead cautions you to pay better attention to the speed limit signs in town. For many people, this warning is enough to remind them to slow down. Next time, you probably won't be so lucky!

There is another way the Five-Step Discipline Process is like the driver's license system. If you haven't had any tickets for some time, many states will expunge your poor driving record and you start all over again from zero. Give your employees a chance to wipe their slate clean, too, if they haven't repeated the infraction for a while. If the second time Chris

IT'S TRUE

During an employee focus group meeting, I asked some new employees about the company's discipline process. One man's response told a sad story about how discipline affects the workplace.

"When I got the job, I was told they were pretty strict about the work rules here. But I've found out differently. One afternoon I was playing basketball with some friends before my shift and got to work 10 minutes late. I thought my manager would come down hard on me, but he didn't say anything about it when I got to work. The next week I wasn't as concerned about getting to work on time because it didn't seem to matter if I was late. No one noticed or cared the last time."

Sometimes it's what management doesn't say or do that makes the strongest impression on a new employee. Fair and consistent discipline at work is not only respected, it is expected.

shows up late happens at least six months after the first time, go back to Step 1 and try that again. The six-month rule works for many infractions that are not serious ones.

The Five-Step Discipline Process works at every level of the organization. It's not just for hourly, front-line employees. Employees at every level can and do break company policies. Ignoring more senior employees' infractions is a dangerous precedent to set. Other employees will know that you have done so, and will resent such favoritism. In addition, you may be disregarding a problem that will become much larger and more time-consuming later.

> " It was character that got us out of bed, commitment that moved us into action, and discipline that enabled us to follow through."
>
> – Zig Ziglar, motivational speaker

For example, think of Chris as a senior executive in the company who is usually one of the first in the office. One day, Chris arrives at work at 10:30, three hours past his usual arrival time. As Chris's boss, you could choose to ignore his lateness the first time. But the fact that it is such unusual behavior for Chris makes it even more important to take note. Call Chris aside and ask him if anything is wrong. "I noticed you were really late today. Is there a problem?" In this way, Step 1 becomes a way to show your concern for Chris. If it happens again soon, move to Step 2. Have the next conversation in your office. You may uncover a personal problem that Chris was reluctant to discuss with you. The first two steps are informal conversations that can often lead to identifying the real issue.

Here's the bottom line for you when you discipline the first time an employee breaks a policy:

◆ Fewer meetings in the office correcting employees' behavior

◆ Possibly rescuing an employee from his or her own destructive behavior

◆ Greater respect from all of your employees who expect equal treatment and adherence to the rules for everyone

Ultimately, the greatest reward comes in the form of greater time savings for you. You will spend less time dealing with disciplinary problems.

Publicize the Five-Step Discipline Process

Make sure employees know about the Five-Step Discipline Process by including it in your company handbook and explaining it briefly to employees at orientation. This way your employees will know exactly what to expect if they break a rule. And if things continue to the point where you must proceed to Step 5, no one is surprised—least of all, the employee. He or she will know that all of the steps were followed and the final step is termination.

Back at the Restaurant...

Alex decided to implement the Five-Step Discipline Process in his restaurant. Two months after Chris was late the first time, he arrives without his name badge. Alex moves to Step 2 and gives Chris his second verbal warning, putting him on notice that he must adhere to company policy. Will this cause Chris to sit up and take notice? Alex isn't sure. But he does feel more confident about making employees understand the need for adhering to company rules and regulations. "It's not as hard to discipline the staff," Alex thinks, "when I have a process to follow and everyone knows I'll be using it."

Alex realizes he is spending much less time each week on employee prob-

lems. Before he started using the Five-Step Discipline Process, every time he let an employee get away with breaking a rule, he had to do extra work to make sure the restaurant ran smoothly. "One bad apple really does affect everyone here," thinks Alex. "I've been spending way too much time trying to clean up problems caused by just a few people."

Summary of Chapter Ten:

Employees want to know what is expected of them. Employees who comply with the rules want to see company standards enforced. Those who test the rules, and their managers' patience, need to have their boundaries set by management.

In many cases, management itself is the only obstacle to an effective discipline process. The act of disciplining someone does not appeal to many of us. But once the mechanics are learned and we see the benefits of the progressive process, our confidence grows.

Understanding the Five-Step Discipline Process ensures that there is no excuse for management to ignore or avoid disciplining an employee. Remember, a five-minute disciplining session today may prevent a larger ordeal in the future, or the need to hire and train a new employee to replace the one you were forced to let go.

Beware of the manager who constantly says, "If I've told him once, I've told him a thousand times" or "She should have known better." Any manager who is constantly repeating rules to employees does not know how to properly manage people or time.

The Five-Step Discipline Process is fair, firm, and effective. Its beauty lies in its simplicity and progressive nature.

> Step 1: Quick verbal warning, in a quiet corner of the workplace (not in the private office)
>
> Step 2: Verbal warning in the manager's private office. Short and sweet, but in private.
>
> Step 3: Written warning. Have another manager or shop steward in the meeting, if appropriate, to show how important the issue has become.

Step 4: One day suspension, preferably with pay. The employee must come back to work the next day with a short plan for improvement.

Step 5: Termination. Five strikes and you're out, after plenty of opportunities to turn the behavior around. And no one is surprised or angry at the outcome, including the employee.

The time savings for you will be immediately apparent when you use the Five-Step Discipline Process. Most infractions will stop after Step 1 or 2. These short conversations are usually sufficient to help your employees understand what behaviors are and are not appropriate in the workplace. When you let the bad behavior drag on for too long without disciplining, you spend far more time cleaning up a bigger problem later.

TIMELESS ADVICE

Discipline is a catalytic process that transforms potential into performance.

CHAPTER 11

The Last Ten Minutes of the Day

"Follow effective action with quiet reflection. From the quiet reflection will come even more effective action."
– Peter Drucker, management consultant

W hen Alex was a cook in the restaurant, he enjoyed watching the clock closing in on the end of his shift. He looked forward to that moment when he would tear out of the parking lot, his oversized car speakers blasting his favorite tunes.

Now, as restaurant manager, "end of shift" is a meaningless phrase for Alex. He has a multitude of restaurant responsibilities to take care of before leaving every day. He follows a closing checklist that takes so much time, he almost runs out the door when the list is finished. Most days when he gets in his car, his heart sinks. Why can't he feel like his workday is done?

"I've been working so hard all day," Alex thinks, "but at the end of it, I'm still thinking about what I didn't get done and what I might have to do tomorrow." Forget the mind-altering music on the ride home. Alex spends his ride worrying about what he didn't do today, and what issues will pounce on him tomorrow. When he arrives home, he thinks, "Tomorrow is another day. I'll just deal with the loose ends then."

After a quick dinner, he spends two hours looking over reports he didn't

155

have a chance to read during the day. He wishes he didn't have to work so much at home in the evening. He'd like to get to the gym more often, and his friends always seem to have more free time than he has. "There must be some way to shut off work at the end of the day," thinks Alex.

Wrap It Up!

Remember the new beginning of your workday? You learned how to perform a 20-Minute Disappearing Act at the start of your day. For twenty minutes, you give yourself the luxury of regrouping and organizing without interference from anyone at work.

At the end of the workday, take time to wrap it up. Ten minutes is sufficient for most people to get closure on their day. These ten minutes are an important investment in you, to end your workday with peace of mind so you will be able to enjoy your time away from work.

How many of us leave work physically, but never seem to stop thinking about it? We are preoccupied with a work-related problem during dinner, when we'd rather be enjoying the family. We bring work home to do in the evening rather than reading the latest novel or our favorite magazine. Forget about knowing the latest shows on television—we never get to watch them, or when we do, we're asleep before the opening credits finish rolling. And hobbies—are you someone who says, "I'll pick up a hobby when I retire?"

A Ten-Minute Wrap-Up is all most people need to complete their day. Retreat to a quiet place where you won't be disturbed. If you're the last one who leaves your workplace, this won't be a problem. If others are around, find a place where you can disappear briefly. Shut your office door, unplug the phone, or just ignore what goes on around you for ten minutes. You have these last four items on your agenda to complete before you can go home for the day.

Item #1: Review Your To-Do's

Look at your To-Do Today list for the last time. Review what was on the list and evaluate how well you completed the tasks you set for yourself hours earlier. Figure out if your day went according to plan or if you were thrown off track by unanticipated events.

Compare what was done to what was planned. This activity may reveal some recurring issues that prevent you from completing your To-Do Today list every day. Maybe your scheduled 45-minute lunch break turned into a 75-minute meeting with a staff member who wanted to talk about a new project. Maybe your twice-daily Management by Walking Around exercise, for which you only budget 30 minutes, actually chews up 45 to 50 minutes. Twenty minutes may not seem like much, but if it happens every day, you could be losing one-third of the five hours you are trying to reclaim. Future To-Do Today lists should be time-adjusted accordingly. A Ten-Minute Wrap-Up today will result in better time management for you tomorrow.

Item #2: Best and Worst of the Day

Think back on the day that is just ending. What was the most regrettable mistake you made today? And to balance out your disappointment, follow that with your biggest achievement of the day. Note them both on your To-Do Today list, and you'll have a running record of what you need to correct and what you're really good at. When you review your old To-Do Today lists, you'll be able to see your growth and know what still needs improvement.

New managers will find this item especially helpful. By logging your wins and losses, you'll have feedback to make adjustments when necessary or to reward yourself for a job well done. Even seasoned executives find it useful to note privately what went right and what went wrong every day. You're only able to manage your time well when you are fully aware of exactly how you spend it.

Item #3: Check That ETD Basket!

Glance over at your ETD (Empty This Day) basket on your desk. If there's still something in it, you can't leave. Complete the job before you go home. Remember, you were the one who made it a priority for today. If it was important earlier, chances are it's just as important now. Do it!

Item #4: Start Tomorrow's To-Dos

Now is the perfect time to begin creating your to-do list for tomorrow. You've reviewed what you were able to complete today, you see the list of projects still open, and it's time to decide what you'll tackle in the morning.

Entries on tomorrow's To-Do Today list will come from at least two sources: today's unfinished tasks, and new tasks that were dreamed up while you conducted business today. Don't worry about making sure everything you need to do tomorrow is on the list for now. You'll polish that list tomorrow during your 20-Minute Disappearing Act, where you'll check it against long-term goals, etc. For now, you're still in work mode, and it's the best time to list those tasks you know you'll be doing tomorrow. It's a cathartic process sometimes called "brain dumping." Getting the task out of your mind and down on paper allows you to close the book on today while creating momentum for tomorrow.

Working at Home

When it comes to doing work at home, our advice is: DON'T. Why not?

◆ Typically, you are not paid to work at home.

◆ Almost certainly, you are not paid enough on the job to sacrifice any of your precious family or sleep time.

◆ Your significant others will feel cheated. You've told them that they are your number one priority, but they always seem to play second fiddle to your work.

◆ No need—you manage your work time so well now there is no reason to take work home.

About Your Briefcase

Please note that the briefcase is not a time-saving tool. One of your objectives in planning and organizing your workload is to eliminate the need to take work home.

Work taken home not only extends the workday beyond reasonable limits, it also negatively impacts the family culture, which inevitably indirectly impacts the workplace. When you pull into your driveway or apartment complex, someone is probably looking forward to seeing you—your dog, your spouse, your mother-in-law (it's possible!), your kids, or your significant other.

Unfortunately, the moment they see that briefcase, their attitude shifts from anticipation to resentment. The irony of this negative reaction to your homework is that you rarely open the briefcase at home. So you're penalized psychologically for something you don't even do.

If you are so insecure about your job that you feel compelled to show your boss that you bring work home, carry your briefcase past his/her office, then out the door, and into the trunk of your car and leave it there. The next morning you can walk it back by your boss's door and everyone will be happy.

For what it's worth, most people say that they rarely open their briefcase even when they bring it home. They admit, "It's a habit" or "just in case . . ." or "I might think of something…" Remember your priorities.

Going Home

Pretend that the ignition switch in your car is the on/off switch between your work life and home life. Once that key is turned, work is off and personal time is on. Use the ride home time as your decompression session. Jettison all thoughts of work. Your Ten-Minute Wrap-Up in the office was designed for this reason—to get your work issues out of your mind and down on paper.

Unlike the drive to work, which we suggested earlier should be considered company time, your ride home is *your* time. Volume up, windows down, let'er rip (within the speed limit of course)!

Workday's Done!

After a few weeks of forcing himself to take a Ten-Minute Wrap-Up at the end of each workday, Alex's spirits are visibly lighter as he leaves work. His bag is lighter, too—in fact, he usually leaves the briefcase at work!

As he waves goodbye to the restaurant's night manager, he is pleased to think back on the tasks he accomplished today. "That was a good decision to buy the new freezing equipment for the kitchen," he thinks. "The chef is going to expand our dessert options now, which should bring in some additional income." He's ready for tomorrow, too, now that he's reviewed his to-do list and knows what's on the horizon.

Alex is off to the gym for an hour, then meeting some friends downtown. Managing his time at work has given him access to more free time outside of work, and he's enjoying the balance in his life. Time management helps him to be more productive on the job and gives him time to participate in other activities he enjoys.

Summary of Chapter Eleven:

Separating work time from non-work time is the wisest time management policy. It's energizing to get away from work and enjoy other activities. But you have to leave work at work.

Taking the last ten minutes of the workday to wrap things up and review the day's events puts closure on the day. Compare your goals for the day with what you actually completed. Draft your to-do list for tomorrow. When you have reviewed the accomplishments of the day and know what's in store for you tomorrow, you'll find you can leave work feeling your job today is done.

How to Wrap Up Your Day:

1. Make sure you have a quiet place at the end of your workday where you're not disturbed.

2. Review your to-do list from today. Compare what you completed to what you had planned to complete, and start tomorrow's to-do list with those items that are still unfinished.

3. Briefly reflect on what went well and what was disappointing today. Then move on.

4. Leave the briefcase at work most days. Your time management skills should be strong enough that you're accomplishing your workload on work time.

5. Leave work and enjoy the rest of your day!

TIMELESS ADVICE

Don't consider "you look tired" a compliment that means you are a hard worker. Regularly working 70 hours a week is nothing to brag about. Truly successful people have balance in their life achieved through adroitly allocating each and every one of their 168 weekly hours.

CHAPTER 12

Reclaim Your Five Hours

"Much may be done in those little shreds and patches of time which every day produces, and which most men throw away."
– Charles Caleb Colton, English cleric and writer

We started this book by promising that you could reclaim five hours each week through improved time management. Our fictional business characters, Logan and Alex, improved their time management skills by adopting the techniques in the book, enabling them to reclaim some of the unproductive time they were squandering during the week.

But how much time can *you* hope to gain by incorporating the lessons in this book into your daily routine? In your real-life situations, how will your week be expanded as more time becomes available to you through improved time management?

Start with the suggestions in Chapters One and Two. Create a personal priority list and post it where you can see it daily to remind you to spend your time working toward your life's priorities. You'll stop wasting time on activities that don't move you toward your goals and start saying no to requests that aren't really important to you. This will undoubtedly add at least **15 minutes each week**.

Running total: 15 minutes

In Chapter Three, you learned how to incorporate the 20-Minute Disappearing Act into your daily routine. So did that add on another 20 minutes to each day?

No—those 20 minutes of organizing your life actually *saves* you time every day. When you are ready for what's in store for you each morning, you won't lose time fending off the piranhas who try to attack you with their issues. We estimate you'll reclaim at least **30 minutes each week** organizing your workday during your 20-Minute Disappearing Act.

Running total: 45 minutes

Chapter Four taught you plenty of techniques to ZAP! the distractions that waste time. In fact, the study by Salary.com referred to in the chapter concluded that you would gain two hours *every day* by implementing the time management techniques that eliminate distractions. That's ten hours a week—twice as much as we expect you to find!

But let's be conservative. Some days you are more successful than others in eliminating distracting influences. So you can probably gain **30 minutes each week** at a minimum if you permanently remove at least three persistent distractions from your workday.

Running total: 1 hour, 15 minutes

In Chapter Five, we gave you the tools you need to finally start making those To-Do Today lists you've been meaning to write for years. Instead of guessing which tasks need to be done every day, now you have a simple method to keep track of them. Best of all, you can cross them off when they're completed and experience that great feeling of accomplishment.

The To-Do Today list is an invaluable organizing tool that saves time for every person who uses one. Another **60 minutes each week** is reclaimed by creating and following your To-Do Today list. With it, you work in a planned, organized manner, and waste far less time trying to figure out what should be your next priority.

Running total: 2 hours, 15 minutes

Chapter Six highlighted the importance of delegating tasks to others. In contrast to those who believe "the only work done right is the work we do ourselves," delegation is the key to effective time management. No one can do it all, nor should they try. An efficient time manager delegates everything possible to staff members who are capable. It's cost-effective, skill-building, and shows your prowess as a manager. Using the Personal Delegation Grid helps document the tasks you successfully delegate to others.

How much time can you reclaim through delegating tasks you used to handle yourself? That depends on how much work you were holding on to that others could perform. But if you consistently and permanently delegate at least four duties that you were previously doing yourself, you'll find a large chunk of time becomes available to you—**45 minutes per week**.

Running total: 3 hours

Along with delegating comes the importance of not taking back the baton, as discussed in Chapter Seven. What's the point of delegating work to employees if you allow them to dump it back on you unfinished? Time you thought you had freed up just gets taken away from you again.

Add another **15 minutes a week** to your total for doing a better job of ensuring that your employees see the job through to completion, and because you now ask them for their solution to a problem before you work to resolve it yourself.

Running total: 3 hours, 15 minutes

Chapter Eight explained a number of techniques to handle meetings more effectively. You will certainly feel you have gained time during those weeks when you hold meetings using these tools. On average, you'll reclaim **30 minutes each week** by planning and conducting meetings that are productive and don't waste time.

Running total: 3 hours, 45 minutes

The amount of time you'll reclaim by recruiting employees using the techniques in Chapter Nine is hard to estimate. You may spend a bit more time in the actual recruitment process now, but you'll more than make up for it in less time wasted on underperforming employees.

We noted that many managers spend up to 90 percent of their time on personnel issues, so time reclaimed through better recruiting could be enormous. You should find at least another **30 minutes each week** by instituting a more thoughtful recruiting process that reduces turnover and results in hiring more effective employees.

Running total: 4 hours, 15 minutes

When it comes to discipline, most managers can add up the hours they spend dealing with employees who break the rules. Chapter Ten's Five-Step Discipline Process greatly reduces the time you need to handle infractions fairly and firmly.

The amount of time each person will reclaim will certainly vary widely depending on the number of employees supervised, but at least **30 minutes each week** can be added to your total by holding employees more accountable through constructive discipline.

Running total: 4 hours, 45 minutes

Taking ten minutes every day to wrap up your day's activities is the final step to managing your time in the workplace. Besides getting you ready for tomorrow, it clears your head so you can move on to whatever you enjoy doing after work.

You're sure to reclaim at least **15 minutes each week** just by implementing this step from Chapter Eleven on a daily basis—not to mention the time you're no longer putting in at home doing work you didn't finish at work!

Final tally: 5 hours reclaimed each week

The most important question now is...What will you do with your extra five hours? My answer: anything you want!

Maybe you'll use the extra time at work. Maybe you'll start writing that children's book you've dreamed about for years. Maybe you'll take your workshop invention to the next level.

Or you'll read some books. Or knit a sweater. Or enjoy a dinner with your family.

Here's the point: you can start taking better control of your life by taking better control of your time. Start using the tools in this book and you'll begin to find your extra hours each week. As our friends Alex and Logan found, it's not hard to improve your time management skills. Just take your first step, then keep going.

After all...**it's about time** you did this for yourself!